Real Things

AN ANTHOLOGY

Real

OF **POPULAR CULTURE**

Things

IN AMERICAN POETRY

Edited by
Jim Elledge and **Susan Swartwout**

Indiana University Press

BLOOMINGTON AND INDIANAPOLIS

This book is a publication of
Indiana University Press
601 North Morton Street
Bloomington, Indiana 47404-3797 USA
www.indiana.edu/~iupress

Telephone orders   800-842-6796
Fax orders   812-855-7931
Orders by e-mail   iuporder@indiana.edu

The paper used in this publication meets the minimum
requirements of American National Standard for Information
Sciences—Permanence of Paper for Printed Library Materials,
ANSI Z39.48-1984.

MANUFACTURED IN THE UNITED STATES OF AMERICA

Library of Congress Cataloging-in-Publication Data

Real things : an anthology of popular culture in American poetry /
   edited by Jim Elledge and Susan Swartwout.
        p.   cm.
     Includes indexes.
     ISBN 0-253-33434-9 (cl : alk. paper). — ISBN 0-253-21229-4 (pa :
alk. paper)
        1. Popular culture—United States—Poetry.   2. American
poetry—20th century.   I. Elledge, Jim, date.   II. Swartwout,
Susan.
PS595.P65R43   1998
811'.54080355—dc21   98–35879

1   2   3   4   5   04   03   02   01   00   99

For David & for Jonathan

Contents

monster poems (handwritten annotation)

[viii]

doll poems

[xi]

Introduction

Over the past few decades, American poetry has been ready and willing to "pop." Poetry written about and around popular culture has become not only a major type of contemporary poetry but also a hip art form. Like Andy Warhol's art, popular-culture poetry accessorizes itself with icons, recurring events, or retold contemporarities that are familiar, favorites, and fun. *Real Things* takes you down the yellow-brick road of late-twentieth-century Americana: the good (Barbie, Superman, Marilyn, Mustangs), the bad (*Gilligan* reruns, King Kong, Frankenstein, blonde ambition), and the ugly side of our culture (TV terror, *Psycho*'s shower).

Popular culture has never held as important a place in poetry as now—so much so that those pop elements of culture often speak the language of the poem, rather than vice versa. For example, you need to have seen a Barbie doll (as we all have) to really "get" a Barbie poem. A poem about a U-Haul crossing Iowa reflects more redundancy and transience if you know that U-Haul dealerships are everywhere and you can see hundreds of their trucks on American highways any given day. The products showcased in this anthology of popular-culture poetry are archaeological relics for the poems and for whoever reads them, even decades from now.

Real Things: An Anthology of Popular Culture in American Poetry is a collection of over 150 poems by more than 130 poets, reflecting the attractions of multicultural Americana object and theme. We chose works from poets representing the wide cultural diversity of the United States, a diversity which intertwines and interacts through the medium of popular culture, derived from a culture that has risen out of the industrial melting pot of generations past. The poets themselves come from a multicultural vista of Native Americans, gays and lesbians, women, Hispanics, African Americans, Asian Americans, and Euro-Americans. Each poet creates a distinct vision of popular culture in America; not every image will be familiar, but all are stimulating.

The poems that we selected are created by both emerging writers and the renowned. Many of the poems have appeared before only in literary journals, and thus have yet to be exposed to a larger audience. We've included poems from a variety of contemporary schools, including beat, postmodern, and L*A*N*G*U*A*G*E poetry.

The audience for poetry about popular culture is highly inclusive, particularly with our contemporary interest in multiculturalism. And the text offers choice, another hallmark of popular culture. For the poetry reader, *Real Things* represents a catalogue of our cultural cornucopia. Instructors using *Real Things* can approach the study of popular-culture poetry by assigning sections according to the poets' ethnic backgrounds or according to the popular culture artifact—such as poems about Superman, rites of passage, music, trademarks, or celebrities.

Popular culture has become its own cult. The word *popular* suggests that it has been accepted by large numbers of people. Rather than considering popular culture only in terms of object—such as a Mickey Mouse watch or Coca-Cola jingles—the concept of popular culture also includes generalized attitudes. By that we mean a perspective on various aspects of life in the late twentieth century, which we've come to accept regardless of whether we have questioned them or not—mass murders, sophisticated dirty politics, an unmitigated loneliness in the midst of crowds. Others might call it the postmodern pastiche, which moves fast and is flooded with so much input one can see our culture as a Big Bleed.

We can extend this idea through history, in that popular culture has been accepted and idealized not only in our time but in the past. For example, Superman has transcended several generations since his landing in America over a half-century ago. In an essay entitled "What

Makes Superman So Darned American?" Gary Engle explains that Superman represents the Eurocentric American Dream. His all-American agenda is that he arrives in a New World, he becomes a success, and he attends to the needs of his community. The destruction of Superman may not come from exposure to kryptonite, but rather to technopoly, defined in 1911 in Frederick Taylor's *The Principles of Scientific Management* as the notion that technical calculation is superior to human judgment and that the world is therefore most efficiently run by technology and its head henchman, the computer. In a world where personal success and attention to community have no value, our red-white-and-blue Superman can't survive, hence the radical changes in costume and abilities that Superman has recently undergone. Superman parallels our own necessary relationship to technology and computers. Like most of us, Superman must attempt to upgrade, to transform in order to survive.

In "Popular Culture: Notes Toward a Definition," Ray B. Browne, the academically hailed king of popular culture, separates popular culture from what he terms "elitist" elements, those cultural elements which exclude others in order to define themselves as worthwhile. Browne defines popular culture as "all those elements of life which are not narrowly intellectual or creatively elitist and which are generally though not necessarily disseminated through the mass media. Popular culture consists of the spoken and printed word, sounds, pictures, objects and artifacts" (245). Although his definition might appear to include all forms of art, Browne differentiates between mass culture and popular culture. He explains that a sense of style and a mastery of artistic skills and conventions separates the popular-culture artist from the mass-culture artist. In other words, mass culture relies upon formula, repetition, and stereotypes, while popular culture delights in the creative alteration of what is accepted (242–43).

In their "Introduction to the Study of Popular Culture: What Is This Stuff That Dreams Are Made Of?" Jack Nachbar and Kevin Lause have created a shopping list of criteria for popular culture in order to describe it. Popular culture, they write, consists of objects, people, and events and is produced with the goal of making money. Popular culture imitates itself, hoping that whatever worked before will work again. It not only reflects our values and beliefs but shapes them as well, creating the "fabric of our everyday lives" (10). This concept can include the capitalist sublime, a feeling of exhilaration in materialist pursuits of buying, selling, creating, destroying that pervades our society. Further, Nachbar and Lause divide popular culture proponents into Classicists and Modernists. Classicists feel that popular culture has been a part of history "as long as there have been groups of people available to be entertained and instructed by its appeal" (11). This view includes as popular culture Greek plays at their inception as well as Shakespeare's popular hits. Modernists, on the other hand, believe that popular culture is of recent origin, citing three prerequisites for its existence: masses, money, and mechanics. The masses reflect large groups of people who make the creation of popular culture possible. In other words, a cultural element can't be truly popular unless masses of people, not just the culturally elite, identify it as such. Disposable income must be available to the middle class, not just the elite. Finally, mechanics, a way to distribute elements of culture to the spending masses, must be in place, a feat which began in the late eighteenth century with the high-speed printing press (11–12). The importance of media mechanics upon the growth of popular culture can't be overestimated. We exist in an America where all the fame and foibles of the nation are exposed live in our living rooms: electronic media have changed the very way we think about culture. In his book *Spirits Hovering Over the Ashes: Legacies of Postmodern Theory*, H. L. Hix notes that "the origins of writing and print were separated by 5,000 years of human culture; television and the pc-editable hand-held video camera by less than fifty" (10). While technological advances are becoming streamlined, consumerism and marketing are at the core of the economics of these changes, creating a burgeoning and evolving popular culture. So pervasive is popular culture that product names become part of our common vocabulary, like "Coke" used in many regions for all forms of carbonated beverage or "Kleenex" used for any type of facial tissue. It is to be expected that popular culture would as comfortably and transparently reside within the language of American poetry.

A certain amount of nostalgia is inherent in the ability of a popular culture artifact to survive. Neither popular acceptance of an element nor its creative appeal are enough to withstand time without some more durable sense of human desire attached to it. What we may want today may seem outdated tomorrow. While the poems in *Real Things* do contain an element of nostalgia, the poetry itself is quite the opposite of the poetry of emotive transcendentalists or self-indulging confessionalists. Rather, the feeling captured by the anthology is one beyond particular celebrities, icons, or other elements. Thylias Moss's poem "An Anointing," for example, celebrates products of popular culture as intimately shared experience, although the precise experiences shared are startling and unique. "Me and Molly," the two-as-one personas of the poem, cite inventive rites of passage as the building blocks of their solid relationship. Instead of the traditional rite of "blood brothers" in which the body is marked by self-inflicted wounds from which blood is intermingled, the female personas trade Kotex, commingling the blood of their marked femininity. They flaunt their solidarity against societal mores; they "Don't care what other people think. We're just glad that they do." Invoking the well-known candy slogan, they are "M and M, melt in your mouth," sweet and smooth.

The relationship between popular culture and the way we think is evidenced through the medium of television, which owns a high rank in popular-culture poetry. In some cases the relationship is parasitic, with TV feeding off culture's flesh. Dorothy Barresi's "When I Think of America Sometimes (I Think of Ralph Kramden)" depicts TV's emulation of domesticity in the 1950s. Yet something more sinister than mere imitation is happening here. The borders of comedy and pain often overlap: Ralph, the main character in the TV show, raises his "truncheon of an arm," fist clenched, in his wife's face to proclaim the now-renowned phrase, "To the moon, Alice!" Although threat is implicit, Ralph's expression is humorous, exaggerated; we cannot seriously believe he would hit her. Even she smirks. And we accept that Alice exists in a tiny, dingy flat with little to do but housekeep that flat, a nightmare if we were to think about it. The poet questions, "But why did we think it was so funny?" On TV, verity is masked in exaggeration; common pain is relieved in laughter. We loved *The Honeymooners* for making us see our own plight as somehow comic.

When domestic violence gained notoriety, situation comedies began to avoid such gags. Physical threats were relegated to drama and cartoons. What became a serious, punishable action in the real world likewise became taboo in comedy on TV. Another parasitic relationship revolves around a persona named Dr. Singh in David Wojahn's "Francis Ford Coppola and Anthropologist Interpreter Teaching Gartewienna Tribesmen to Sing 'Light My Fire,' Philippine Jungle, 1978." Dr. Singh appears, on the one hand, as the noble protector of the tribesmen who are being used as extras in the filming of *Apocalypse Now*. He insists on short work hours for them so that their annual pig hunt can take place as usual the next day. On the other hand, paramount in Dr. Singh's mind is the Mercedes SL that he will purchase with his consulting fee, a major impetus to his version of "the show must go on." Yet even the locals profit from the film, with "Brando signing glossies for the witch doctor / To grind into aphrodisiacs." Instead of the media changing to parallel the culture, as in *The Honeymooners*, here the culture adapts itself to the presence and commercial benefits of the media.

At other times, the relationship between thought and popular culture is symbiotic. The symbiotic relationship often works in mysterious yet marketable ways, such as the phenomenon of the talk show, which creates a chicken-or-egg situation with popular culture. What comes first: oddity or our rabid desire to hear about it? Albert Goldbarth addresses several of the prevalent issues in his poem "The Talk Show." A woman hears angels speaking through her body, but the truth uncovered is that her IUD picks up police-band radio. A mechanic with the nickname "Dude Man" becomes the conductor for a mysterious force that enters through his wrench and exits through his hand "out / its guttering candelabrum fingers and into / the frame of the Ford." This mechanic's miracle coincides with the full moon, that icon of lunacy and supernatural beings, "while the universe hums / its lunar kazoo, and adrenalin everywhere dervishes." The piper's pay here, however, is a spot on national TV, whose ratings prove we are all accomplices in this facet of our popular culture. David Trinidad illustrates the symbiosis through both his subject matter and his structure in "The Shower Scene in *Psycho*." Frames from the movie *Psycho* are alternated with real-life horrors: the Manson family murders and the fascination of the poem's speaker with those horrors. The poem analyzes the attraction—not only of the speaker but of all of us—to violent death. When the speaker of the poem is confronted by his mother, who has discovered his collection of clippings about murders, we are all caught in the paradoxical spotlight of our morbid fascination and our repulsion toward spilled blood. The structure of the poem links one partner in crime with the other, as codependent as our attraction and our fear.

Three other poems entwine popular culture with who we are, or who we think we are. Lucille Clifton's "note, passed to superman" expresses the understanding of the speaker for Superman's disguise as a necessary defense on a strange planet. The speaker understands masks, stating "there is no planet stranger / than the one I'm from." Superman mirrors the speaker's dilemma: the issue of identity in a world that reacts to one's outer appearance. In "Never Land" by Yusef Komunyakaa, the issue of identity magnifies Michael Jackson, a nouveau Frankenstein and monster in one, "so eager / to play The Other" that he has disappeared inside a distant simulacrum of self. So confused has his identity become that the poet must remind Jackson that no matter "what the makeup artist / says, you know // your sperm will never / reproduce that face." The perfectly proportioned, culturally celebrated face that Michael Jackson has evolved himself into is a freak of culture, not of nature. In a sense, popular culture performs the surgery. The poem calls attention to the scars.

Somewhere, sometime today, you'll see someone wearing a T-shirt with an icon of popular culture on it. The various products of America and their jingles are a part of our lives, so much so that we wear them on our clothing, buy them as status symbols, and hum the persistent tunes unaware. *Real Things* gives the reader the pleasure of seeing Americana with new eyes, the eyes of a traveler through the medium of poetry into a familiar and frolicking world of real things.

WORKS CITED

Browne, Ray B. "Popular Culture: Notes Toward a Definition." *Eye on the Future: Popular Culture Scholarship into the Twenty-first Century.* Ed.

Marilyn Motz et al. Bowling Green, Ohio: Bowling Green State University Popular Press, 1994. 239–45.

Engle, Gary. "What Makes Superman So Darned American?" *Superman at Fifty: The Persistence of a Legend.* Ed. Dennis Dooley and Gary Engle. Cleveland: Octavia Press, 1987.

Hix, H. L. *Spirits Hovering over the Ashes: Legacies of Postmodern Theory.* Albany: State University of New York Press, 1995.

Nachbar, Jack, and Kevin Lause. *Popular Culture: An Introductory Text.* Bowling Green, Ohio: Bowling Green State University Popular Press, 1992.

Taylor, Frederick. *The Principles of Scientific Management.* London: Harper, 1911.

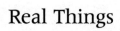

Real Things

REGINALD SHEPHERD

Hygiene

Some men wash their hands five times a day
and still feel dirty. Some hands can never be
clean enough. In this town everyone's still talking
about Jeffrey Dahmer. It's fifty degrees at noon
in May, Milwaukee, 1993, city of cream
bricks and Miller beer.
                              Last night I took home a man
whose best friend Dahmer killed. Black gays
called him "The Sniper." Families filed missing person
reports, neighbors complained about strange smells. Men still
went home with him. "For a lot of black guys it's a treat
to get to sleep with a white man." He found them
at the Grand Avenue Mall, or at the no longer popular
Club 219, where white men go to pick up
black men. His building's been torn down
(Oxford Apartments, number 213), a fenced-in
empty lot in a black neighborhood
just blocks from downtown: you can't see it
from there. Eleven skulls, one skeleton,
a freezer stocked with assorted
body parts. They found bones
in the basement they still can't identify. Every
blond man in town looks like him. His
more than a hundred pages of confession mention
"my consuming lust to experience
their bodies." Every white man in Milwaukee.

It's late May, 1993, it's thirty degrees
at night.
        A man naked in bed beside you has a smell
that's quite particular, not unpleasant but
distinct. It stays in the room all morning
after he's gone, you don't know where
it comes from. Dead bodies have a smell also
which some men will do anything
to understand. An experiment
in how close you can get
to someone else. "Mass murderers
are men who can't control their interest
in other people." They're men consumed
by curiosity. Close enough to get inside
his skin, to take his smell and make it
yours. Just three of them were white, the seventeen
men and boys he killed, dismembered, sometimes
ate. They couldn't get the smell
out of the building. An experiment
in how to become someone else
who isn't moving anymore.

JUNE JORDAN

Mid-Year Report: For Haruko

By this time
20,000 Tutsi had been slaughtered
by Hutus using machetes
and I could not remember exactly the last time
I held you in my arms

By this time
it was hot where you live
and foggy and cool where I
sat working away on songs
about romance more daily
than fat free
cappucino

By this time
100% cotton tee shirts for O.J. Simpson sold
really well at twelve dollars
a pop and
his swell new girl friend
swore
he never
ever
hit her

By this time
you were farming trees
for Christmas
in the middle of July

while I was taking flowers
out of the garden
and putting in stones
and rocks
and boulders

By this time
O.J. Simpson hired ten attorneys
each of them a flat fee candidate
for half a million dollars
and
by this time
nobody could name the children
of Nicole

By this time
200,000 Tutsi had been slaughtered
by Hutu homicidal maniacs
and not one European
and not one African
and not one Asian
and not one U.S. of A. anybody
had done
one
single thing
to intervene

By this time
American Armed Force Commanders argued
about whether or not
the U.N. owed them money
for parts to helicopters
that (anyway) left the States
too late
to mitigate the magnitude
to mitigate the gross

indignities
and terror
of Rwandan genocide

By this time
O.J. Simpson walked
"thumbs up" into court
and congress passed a 30 billion dollar
crime bill
irrelevant to female loneliness
inside the legal violence
of in-house
abuse

By this time
I couldn't look
anymore
at old photographs of your body
soft against the trees
about to fall
and
I couldn't look
anymore
at new photographs of babies
pulling at the arms
of dead mothers and dead brothers
nobody in Africa
nobody in Europe
nobody in Asia
nobody in these United States
gave a shit
about

By this time
I was reading your letters
all by myself

again
and I could not remember exactly the last time
I held you in my arms

Oh my love

The extinction of a people
The extinction of a life
The extinction of a love
is
like I cannot
remember what

exactly

LUCI TAPAHONSO

Pay Up or Else

Vincent Watchman was shot
in the head February 12
because he owed 97¢ at
        a Thriftway gas station.

While he lay dead,
the anglo gas boy said
        I only meant to shoot out
        his car tires and scare him.
He fired 2 poor shots—one in the head,
        one in the rear window and
the police cited him for
shooting a firearm within city limits.

Meanwhile, Thriftway officials in Farmington
expressed shock
        It's not company policy, after all,
        to shoot Navajo customers who run
        overflows in the self-serve pumps.
        This man will definitely be fired.

        There is no way that such an action
        can be justified, the official said

while we realized our lives weren't worth a dollar
        and a 24-year-old Ganado man never used
        the $3 worth of gas he paid for.

JONATHAN HOLDEN

Why We Bombed Haiphong

When I bought bubble gum
to get new baseball cards
the B-52 was everywhere you looked.
In my high school yearbook
the B-52 was voted "Most Popular"
and "Most Likely to Succeed."

The B-52 would give you the finger
from hot cars. It laid rubber,
it spit, it went around in gangs,
it got its finger wet and sneered
about it. It beat the shit
out of fairies.

I remember it used to chase
Derek Remsen around at recess
every day. Caught, he'd scream
like a girl. Then the rest
of us pitched in and hit.

DAVID TRINIDAD

The Shower Scene in *Psycho*

She closes the bathroom door to secure her privacy, slips off her robe, drapes it over the toilet bowl, steps into the bath, and closes the shower curtain behind her, filling the frame with a flash of white (5.89).

Shortly before midnight on Friday, August 8, 1969, Manson called together Family members Tex Watson, Susan Atkins, Patricia Krenwinkel, and Linda Kasabian to give them their instructions.

From Marion viewed through the translucent shower curtain, Hitchcock cuts to (5.90), framed from within the space bounded by the curtain. At the top center of this frame is the shower head.

Fortified with drugs and armed with a gun, knives, rope, and wire cutters, they were to take one of the Family cars and go to 10050 Cielo Drive in Beverly Hills.

Marion rises into the frame. Water begins to stream from the shower head. She looks up into the stream of water and begins to wash her neck and arms. Her expression is ecstatic as the water brings her body to life (5.91).

In the secluded ranch-style house at the end of the cul-de-sac, Sharon Tate, aged twenty-six, a star of *Valley of the Dolls* and now eight and a half months pregnant, was entertaining three guests: Hollywood hair stylist Jay Sebring, coffee heiress Abigail Folger, and Folger's lover Voytek Frykowski.

At this point, there is a cut to Marion's vision of the shower head, water radiating from it in all directions like a sunburst (5.92).

(I had just turned sixteen, was about to start my last year at Chatsworth High.)

Hitchcock cuts to the shower head viewed from the side (5.93) at the precise moment Marion turns her naked back to the stream of water.

(Every Saturday, I went to the matinee at the Chatsworth Cinema.)

Marion takes pleasure in the stream of water emanating from the shower head (5.94).

(The theater was next to the Thrifty Drug where, two summers before, I'd bought a copy of *Valley of the Dolls*.)

From the side view of the shower head, Hitchcock cuts back to Marion, still ecstatic (5.95). Then he cuts to a setup that places the camera where the tile wall of the shower "really" is.

(I took it home and hid it under my bed. I knew it was the kind of book my mother wouldn't let me read.)

The shower curtain, to which Marion's back is turned, hangs from a bar at the top of the screen, and forms a frame-within-a-frame that almost completely fills the screen (5.96).

(The summer before that, she'd found the box of newspaper clippings on the top shelf of my closet.)

The camera begins to move forward, until the bar at the top becomes excluded from the screen (5.97).

(For weeks, I'd been cutting out articles about murders.)

Synchronized with this movement of the camera, Marion slides out of the frame, so that the shower curtain completely fills the screen (5.98).

(It started with the eight nurses in Chicago. Right after that was the Texas sniper. Then there was the politician's daughter who was bludgeoned and stabbed to death in her sleep.)

A shadowy figure, barely visible through the shower curtain, enters the door that can just be made out in the background. It steps forward toward the camera, its form doubled by and blending into its shadow cast on the translucent curtain (5.99).

After cutting telephone wires to the house, they gained access to the property by scaling fences, careful not to set off alarms.

The curtain is suddenly wrenched open and a silhouetted knife-wielding figure is revealed (5.100).

As they walked up the drive, a car approached from the house and caught them in its headlights.

The silhouetted figure is symmetrically flanked by the raised knife on the one side and the light bulb on the other (5.101).

At the wheel was eighteen-year-old Steven Parent, who had been visiting the caretaker, William Garretson. In his apartment over the garage, Garretson listened to his stereo with headphones on, unaware of what was happening just yards away.

When the camera reverses field to Marion, turned away (5.102), her figure displaces the silhouette in (5.101).

Parent slowed down and asked who they were, and what they wanted.

It is through the silhouetted figure's eyes that Marion is now viewed, as she turns around clockwise until she looks right into the camera (5.103). What she sees makes her open her mouth to scream.

Watson's response was to place the barrel of a .22 against the youth's head and blast off four rounds.

Jump cut to a closer view of Marion's face (5.104).

(I didn't know why I was so fascinated by murder.)

Second jump cut to an extreme close-up of her wide-open mouth (5.105).

(I told my mother the clippings were "research," that one day I wanted to write about crime. She made me throw them away.)

From Marion's point of view, the silhouetted figure strikes out violently with its knife (5.106).

Watson slit one of the window-screens, crawled into the house, and admitted the others through the front door. Linda Kasabian remained outside as lookout.

The knife slashes down for the first time (5.107).

Frykowski, who was asleep on a sofa in the living room, woke up to find Watson standing over him, gun in hand.

The knife slashes through the corner of the screen. The arm and the knife remain silhouetted (5.108).

Atkins reported to Watson that there were three more people in the house. He ordered her to bring them into the living room, which she did at knife-point.

In a slightly closer variant of (5.107), the knife is again raised, its blade gleaming in the light.

(The first time I saw *Psycho*, I was baby-sitting for a couple who lived at the end of a dark cul-de-sac.)

This shot frames part of Marion's body along with the intruder's arm, still shadowy in the frame (5.109).

(I prayed they'd stay out late. I wouldn't have been allowed to watch it at home.)

Viewed from overhead, the shower-curtain bar cuts across the screen. As Marion tries to fend it off, the knife strikes three times (5.110).

(There was a storm that night: rain and branches beat against the windows. I waited anxiously for "The Late Show" to come on.)

Marion's face fills the screen, expressing bewilderment and pain (5.111).

(They'd cut most of the shower scene for TV.)

Marion holds onto the shadowy arm as it weaves three times in a spiraling movement (5.112).

(I felt cheated.)

Reprise of (5.111).

(I wanted to be scared.)

Reprise of (5.112).

When Sebring was told to lie face down on the floor, he tried to grab Watson's gun, whereupon Watson shot him through the lung.

Another variant of (5.107). The knife again slashes down.

Watson looped one end of a nylon rope around Sebring's neck, threw the free end over a beam and tied it around the necks of Folger and Tate, who had to stand upright to avoid being choked.

Marion turns her face away, her head almost sliding out of the frame (5.113).

Watson ordered Atkins to stab Frykowski, who got to his feet and ran outside. Atkins pursued him onto the lawn, and knifed him in the back.

[13]

The slashing knife (5.114).

Watson followed, shot Frykowski twice and, when his gun jammed, continued to beat him over the head with the butt.

A shot of Marion recoiling, still bewildered (5.115).

In the living room, the two women struggled to free themselves from their dual noose.

This shot approximates (5.114), but this time the knife slashes through the center of the frame.

Like Frykowski, Folger got as far as the front lawn. She was chased down by Krenwinkel, who stabbed her repeatedly.

Reprise of (5.115). Marion's bewildered reaction.

Watson also descended upon her, after first knifing Sebring.

The hand and knife come into clear focus. Water bounces off the glinting metal of the blade (5.116).

Then they turned on the heavily pregnant Miss Tate.

Juxtaposition of blade and flesh (5.117).

(In secret, I read *Valley of the Dolls* several times.)

Marion recoils, but still looks dazed, entranced (5.118).

(My mother found my hiding place and made me throw the book away.)

A low-angle view facing the door. The knife slashes through the frame (5.119).

(I bicycled to Thrifty Drug, bought another copy, and snuck it into the house.)

Marion's back and arms. The intruder's arm again enters the frame (5.120).

Watson told Atkins to stab her.

Closeup of Marion's face. She is now clearly in agony (5.121).

When the actress begged to be spared for the sake of her un-born child, Atkins sneered, "Look, bitch, I don't care . . . "

Blood drips down Marion's writhing legs (5.122).

"I have no mercy for you."

Marion turns her face from the camera. The knife enters the frame (5.123).

She hesitated nonetheless, so Watson inflicted the first wound.

Reprise of (5.122), with a greater flow of blood.

Within moments, Atkins and Krenwinkel joined in, stabbing her sixteen times.

The screen flashes white as the camera momentarily frames only the bare tile wall. Marion's hand, viewed from up close and out of focus, enters and then exits the frame (5.124).

Finally, Susan Atkins dipped a towel in Sharon Tate's blood and wrote the word "Pig" on the front door.

The intruder exists (5.125).

It was not until the next day, when they watched TV at the Spahn Movie Ranch in Chatsworth, that any of them knew who they had murdered.

Marion's hand pressed against the white tile (5.126). It slowly slides down the wall.

(The same summer I read *Valley of the Dolls*, the book was being made into a movie.)

Marion's hand drops out of the frame and her body slowly slides down the wall. She turns to face forward as her back slips down, the camera tilting down with her (5.127).

(After Patty Duke, my childhood idol, was cast in one of the lead roles, it was practically all I could think about.)

She looks forward and reaches out, as if to touch someone or something she cannot see (5.128). The camera pulls slowly away. Then her hand changes its path.

(I made a scrapbook of pictures I had clipped from movie magazines:)

In extreme close-up, Marion's hand continues its movement until it grasps the shower curtain in the left foreground of the frame (5.129).

(Patty reaching for a bottle of pills, tears streaming down her face;)

The shower curtain, unable to bear her weight, pulls away from the supporting bar, as the hooks give way one by one (5.130).

(Barbara Parkins in a white bathrobe, collapsed on the beach;)

Marion's arm falls, followed by her head and torso. Her body spills over from within the shower, and lands on the curtain (5.131).

(Sharon Tate in a low-cut beaded dress, her blonde hair piled up high.)

From (5.131), there follows a cut to the reprise of the sunburst shot of the shower head viewed frontally.

(Later, when the movie premiered at Grauman's Chinese, I begged my mother to take me to see it.)

The camera cuts to Marion's legs, blood mixing with the water (5.132), and begins to move to the left, following this flow of water and blood.

("Wait till it comes to the Chatsworth Cinema," she said.)

At the moment Marion's legs are about to pass out of the frame, the drain comes into view (5.133).

(The Saturday the bodies were discovered, I saw *Mackenna's Gold*, a Western starring Omar Sharif and Gregory Peck.)

The camera reframes to center the drain as it tracks in toward it, so that the blackness within appears about to engulf the screen (5.134).

(The "Coming Attraction" was for *Goodbye, Columbus,* a serious adult drama.)

At this point, there is a slow dissolve from the drain to an eye, viewed in extreme close-up (5.135).

(The following week I would ride up to see it, but they wouldn't let me in. It was recommended for mature audiences.)

This eye, which fixes the camera in its gaze, displaces the drain in the frame, and appears to peer out from within it (5.136).

(We lived a few miles from the Spahn Movie Ranch.)

The camera spirals out clockwise as though unscrewing itself, disclosing the eye, Marion's, dead (5.137).

(There was a newspaper machine in front of the Chatsworth Cinema. I always chained my bicycle to it.)

The camera keeps spiraling out until we have a full view of Marion's face (5.138).

(When I left the theater that afternoon, I saw the face of Sharon Tate.)

Death has frozen it in inexpressiveness, although there is a tear welled in the corner of her eye (5.139).

(Then I read the headline as my eyes adjusted to the sun.)

KATHARYN HOWD MACHAN

No, Superman Was Not the Only One

for Bridget and Meg

In secret, Lois Lane wore coins and jewels
draped perfectly against the naked skin
she perfumed with wild jasmine, taunting fools
who'd denigrate her dance as snaky sin.
She called for drumbeat, shook the stage apart
with shift and shimmy, crescent arms upraised
to show the world the power of her art
and how on Earth the Goddess should be praised.
In silvered silk, her pinned-up hair set free,
she swayed and turned and seemed almost to fly
above the smoky air, almost to be
a bird, a plane, super in midnight sky.
No newspaper reported what she did;
even from Clark she kept her cimbals hid.

LUCILLE CLIFTON

note, passed to superman

sweet jesus, superman,
if i had seen you
dressed in your blue suit
i would have known you.
maybe that choirboy clark
can stand around
listening to stories
but not you, not with
metropolis to save
and every crook in town
filthy with kryptonite.
lord, man of steel,
i understand the cape,
the leggings, the whole
ball of wax.
you can trust me,
there is no planet stranger
than the one i'm from.

RAFAEL CAMPO

Superman Is Dead

I used to think that immortality
Was just like Superman, without the tights
And cape—just flying naked through the sky,
As muscled as the clouds, able to leap
Tall buildings in a single bound. I thought
To be invincible was what it meant—
To live forever! I was innocent.
Back then, I hadn't learned the words they taught,
Like hemochromatosis, kryptonite.
And now, I wonder whether words do weigh
Upon the soul. I wonder if I say
Your name urgently enough at night,
Might you descend and hold me in your arms
Again, like Superman but naked, free
And muscled as the clouds, able to leap
Back into bed, your body hard and warm.

If I Were Rita Hayworth

I would hear Spanish first.
My father would teach me how to shimmer.
My mother would keep her mouth shut.

I would wear red dresses at age 12
and dance like a woman many years older.
I would dance in my father's arms.

Later I would dye my hair red
and pluck the last Spanish words from my mouth.

I would masquerade as an American—
that healthy girl next door who knows
how to crack a whip.

I would dream only in black and white
(after Technicolor, some peace is needed).

As the Studio built a whole world for me
full of fresh cream and gingerbread, I would seek
out the darkest men, nigger dark, then fuck them
into marriage. I would wed a Prince of Darkness
and bear daughters named for the perfumes of Arabia.
If I were Rita Hayworth, strung between living a lie
and bearing a sickness so furious it ages me to dream of it,
I would rage in my illness, make a black hole
wide enough to swallow the damnation of my beauty.

KATHLEEN DE AZEVEDO

Famous Women—
Claudette Colbert

He was quite a guy how he laughed like oh what's the name of the guy
He said dude he said babe he said dude he said babe
Just as a stork flew by
Like he knows which is which?

The treatment: Who's to know which is which?

It was a warm Hollywood night
Tongue hanging warmth
The kinda warmth that makes asphalt turn into grainy black hair
The kind Claudette Colbert wore in oh what's the name of the movie

The studio got him a dummy and oh what a dummy
Someone stuck Claudette Colbert into the trunk of his Olds
Really cruel people, the kind you don't want to meet
Stuck her in his trunk
Really cruel people played a trick on a starry-eyed kid
Initiated for the first time on the LA freeway
The entrances and exits and all the guys behind you laughing
Kinda makes you nervous

How about exploding palm trees!
How about the stork carrying newborn dudes and babes to Universal!
It kinda makes you nervous the first time out
Kinda like how it felt with oh what was the name of that girl

So away he went doing wheelies down the Santa Monica
This was the great love affair of the Western World

He and Claudette chugging on a steamy evening oh so steamy until
The back of the trunk burst into flames like palm trees
Kinda made him nervous

He pulled to the side and fanned the flames
But it was too hot, baby
So he started thumbing for a ride
Like Clark Gable in oh what's the name of that—

It's plastic now.
The back of the Olds, Claudette was plastic after all a plastic dummy
Kinda makes you nervous, huh?
Plasticky melted fleshy bubbly poly peptide urethane all over the
chrome bumper sloppy on the license plate tail lights
A big plastic fleshy mess, the whole back of the Olds looks like
a big fleshy ass

Which is which?

What a sight for such a new boy in town
A faceless new boy new born
The stork carried him
Things like that always happen here
Never got real famous but close enough and at least he was happy
Not that we can tell which was which

BILL KUSHNER

Up

This? it's my Lounge Lizard look, very
popular in the 20's when I was but a thought
whether Flying Down to Rio or crossing Mulberry
I am I suppose what I was always meant to be
a slight eccentric with a bit of a tic
a sort of a gay Mary Poppins so thank you dear
America you've got taste you've got style
& you know a good drag queen when you see one
she sure can talk & she thanks everybody & I'm
so happy that 2000 years ago sweet Jesus died
for me, including my girlfriend Judy up there
in Canada & like to thank my mother & my father
for putting up with my noise all these many years I
love & thank you all for the best performance by a male

SUSAN SWARTWOUT

The Gypsy Teaches
Her Grandchild Wolfen Ways

All tongues tell their monsters, shapes
that shift from human to hell   under bridges
and beds: woman crouches to carnivore
or man twists to fiend. They leave howls
inside you forever.

But werewolf's a charmer, mouth full
of bone-glint, handsome
as a polished gun   all sass and Satan.
Stars flicker in wolfen smiles like light
off a knife blade   hard
under soft lips.

                        Werewolf chases
the red ride in your heart   beams
radar eyes to track blood's hot
dance. You turn   wolf's on you—
wants you for your organs   you,
Fool, who brings kibble and collar.

Sometimes in blue moon's night
werewolf sulks   mourns   lonely in self's
heartless shadow.   For a moment
werewolf trades murder's sweet drink
for a soul   silver voice to warn you
with cries like rabbits sobbing before death.

Now you think, *I can bewitch the beast,*
grasp handfuls of fur, pull wolf through you
as if your heart's a hoop.
　　　　　Turn again, child;
pray the gleam shines from faith not fang.

C O N N I E   D E A N O V I C H

Frankenstein

Frankenstein naps on a golden bed
covered by a floral quilt
handstitched as he is handstitched

He dreams of making a gigantic sandwich
the tense moment of triumph coming when finally
he gets both hands to work at once

He dreams of picnicking in a glistening meadow
recently cleaned by a biology class
dreams of riding there on top a glistening Harley

He sees himself this way or else
prone in black leather
glamorously handcuffed inside his electric dungeon

Tomorrow he'll rise arms first from his golden bed
trying to piece together the images of his dreams
into an incontestable memory

When he stumbles toward you
will you slowly teach him your name
or will you quickly distribute fire?

[handwritten annotations: learn what you don't understand or find strange (other culture) or shun it / destroy it?]

EDWARD FIELD

The Bride of Frankenstein

The Baron has decided to mate the monster,
to breed him perhaps,
in the interests of pure science, his only god.

So he goes up into his laboratory
which he has built in the tower of the castle
to be as near the interplanetary forces as possible,
and puts together the prettiest monster-woman you ever saw
with a body like a pin-up girl
and hardly any stitching at all
where he sewed on the head of a raped and murdered beauty
      queen.

He sets his liquids burping, and coils blinking and buzzing,
and waits for an electric storm to send through the equipment
the spark vital for life.
The storm breaks over the castle
and the equipment really goes crazy
like a kitchen full of modern appliances
as the lightning juice starts oozing right into that pretty corpse.

He goes to get the monster
so he will be right there when she opens her eyes,
for she might fall in love with the first thing she sees as
      ducklings do.
That monster is already straining at his chains and slurping,
ready to go right to it:
He has been well prepared for coupling

by his pinching leering keeper who's been saying for weeks,
"Ya gonna get a little nookie, kid,"
or "How do you go for some poontang, baby?"
All the evil in him is focused on this one thing now
as he is led into her very presence.

She awakens slowly,
she bats her eyes,
she gets up out of the equipment,
and finally she stands in all her seamed glory,
a monster princess with a hairdo like a fright wig,
lightning flashing in the background
like a halo and a wedding veil,
like a photographer snapping pictures of great moments.

She stands and stares with her electric eyes,
beginning to understand that in this life too
she was just another body to be raped.

The monster is ready to go:
He roars with joy at the sight of her,
so they let him loose and he goes right for those knockers.
And she starts screaming to break your heart
and you realize that she was just born:
In spite of her big tits she was just a baby.

But her instincts are right—
rather death than that green slobber:
She jumps off the parapet.
And then the monster's sex drive goes wild.
Thwarted, it turns to violence, demonstrating sublimation
        crudely;
and he wrecks the lab, those burping acids and buzzing coils,
overturning the control panel so the equipment goes off like
        a bomb,
and the stone castle crumbles and crashes in the storm
destroying them all . . . perhaps.

Perhaps somehow the Baron got out of that wreckage of his
    dreams
with his evil intact, if not his good looks,
and more wicked than ever went on with his thrilling career.
And perhaps even the monster lived
to roam the earth, his desire still ungratified;
and lovers out walking in shadowy and deserted places
will see his shape loom up over them, their doom—
and children sleeping in their beds
will wake up in the dark night screaming
as his hideous body grabs them.

BARBARA HAMBY

St. Clare's Underwear

You can see why men are such monsters
   when you look at a woman's body,
Devonshire creamy from a bath,
   or just the general curviness
   of the whole design.
Then there's your average man,
   hirsute and raging with testosterone,
Godzilla *incarnato*, King Kong with big feet,
   Frankenstein hovering
over some delectable damsel with skin
   like fresh pastry.
So you can see why St. Clare threw in her lot
   with St. Francis, a nice guy,
   good with animals,
although there were rumors. But aren't there
   always?
In Italian, the word for noise is *rumore*,
   which is what gossip is,
though why women should be thought
   more inclined to tittle-tattle than men
   is a mystery to me,
but not something I was thinking about
   one evening in Florence
   as my husband and I strolled
   along the Lungarno Soderini
and in the Piazza Cestello happened upon

a theatre presenting Goldoni's
The Gossip of Women,
though after one act I felt that it could have
as easily been called *The Foppery of Men.*
My dear, the prancing and smirking
that transpired,
and in a country known for its machismo.
When the young lover puckered his carmine lips,
the men in the audience were making a noise
that sounded for all the world like laughter,
though one can never be certain.
I learned something that night,
though exactly what, I'm not sure,
and my education continued in Assisi
where we saw glass cases with the clothes
of St. Francis and St. Clare,
sandals and sackcloth,
though Clare's case contained what looked like
a rough slip or chemise.
"St. Clare's underwear," I cried with such happiness
to my husband,
but by that point he was sick of me
and my non-Catholic lack of respect for everything
he no longer holds dear.
In Italy you are either *cattolico* or *acattolico,*
which, I imagine, makes Anglicans
and Four-Square Gospel Pentecostals
rather uneasy bed partners,
as, I suppose, hermaphrodites and transsexuals
are made anxious by the words
"woman" and "man."
I like to think of Kierkegaard's idea
of the natural home of despair
being in the "heart of happiness,"
which could mean any number of things,

such as black is not black or even white,
or that we are all as confused as Dracula,
      dreaming of a local milkmaid, her C-cup,
      coarse lingerie, ruddy cheeks,
and the blood, of course, always the blood.

*

WILLIAM TROWBRIDGE

Kong Breaks a Leg
at the William Morris Agency

First, this one: "Peetah, Peetah, Peetah!"
said up on my toes, taking tiny steps,
with lots of shoulder. Then, eyes fluttering,
"Ah have ahlways depended on the kahndness
of stranghas." Finale with ruby slippers,
heels clicking, eyes vague, "There's no place
like home, there's no place like home,
there's no. . . ." They said these wouldn't do:
too passé, not enough oom-pa-pa, that I needed
to butch it up a little, surprise them,
go for the blockbuster, the dynamite finish.
These words stung like bullets, but I told
myself to be a trouper, to break many legs.
"Imagine you're Pearl Harbor," I said inscrutably.

Fischer essay

DAVID WOJAHN

Francis Ford Coppola and Anthropologist Interpreter Teaching Gartewienna Tribesmen to Sing "Light My Fire," Philippine Jungle, 1978

It's done phonetically, of course, at great
Expense. Dr. Singh, the bull-horned anthropologist,

Struts with Francis on the peopled set, insists
On short hours for the warriors, who must hunt

Wild pig tomorrow, an annual ritual
That should not be disturbed.
                                        But integrity

Matters less to him than his large consulting fee.
Back in Manila, he will buy a Mercedes SL

And forget about the Leader's new doubleknits,
Leader's Number-Three-Wife
                                        snorting coke with Dennis Hopper,

Brando signing glossies for the witch doctor
To grind into aphrodisiacs.

                    CAW-MAWN   BAY-BE   LIGHT   *Come on baby light my fire*

MY FOY-OR they chant.
                    "What mean *Apocalypse Now*?" asks Leader.

Dr. Singh: "Mean: *everybody-die-together-here.*"

Contrast of values

[35]

colonial condensation(?)

— one culture destroying another under firepower

DIANE MEI LIN MARK

Suzie Wong Doesn't Live Here

Suzie Wong
doesn't live here anymore
yeah, and
Madame Butterfly
and the geisha ladies have all
gone
to
lunch (hey, they might
    be gone a very
    long
    time)

no one here
but
ourselves

      stepping on,
without downcast eyes,
without calculating dragon power,
without tight red cheongsams
  embroidered with peonies
without the
silence
that you've come to
know so well
and we,
to feel so alien with

[handwritten margin note: old cultures now gone / not in USA]

seeing each other at last
so little needs to be explained

there is this strength

born female in Asian America,
our dreams stored years
in the backrooms
of our minds

now happening—
like sounds of flowers
bathed in noontime light
reaching righteously skyward!

*culture is taught? –
there – learned?
seen?*

Suzy Wong's Been Dead a Long Time

a friend calls, says,
after an Unbound Feet performance
she cried,
seeing for the first time in forty years
her own face on stage,
her father's voice in my play.
hears for the first time
about experiences so close to her own.

she says she never
experienced any racism
growing up yellow in Walnut Creek.
but after the show
three men trailed her,
a woman alone,
walking down University Avenue.

stereotype

hey, you Oriental pussycat,
c'mon over here, Suzy Wong.

when she picked up speed,
crossed the street,
they yelled,

wouldn't fuck you no way,
flat face,
slant eye.

spite

a friend calls, says,
i'm real depressed,
even thought about suicide.
can't find a job,
can't pay the rent,
got a dollar in the bank
and thirty cents in my pocket.
even thought about posing
for porno pictures.

i say,
don't hang up, hang in.
you are not alone.
do not walk alone
into the eye of the lens — *public*
to be beaten, raped,
tortured and mutilated.
do not walk alone
into the eye of the lens.

women walk together,
transform our tears   *union*
and our rage into action.
chant, scream, shout:

hey mister,
i ain't your pussycat,   *yeh!*
bitch or broad.
quit calling me chickie,
cutie, fox or floozy.
i'm too old to be baby
or the little lady,
and i ain't Miss Dragon Lady

and Suzy Wong's been dead a long time.

CHRYSTOS

Soap Bubbles

When I was in high school, I wanted to be an actress.
I could cry on demand, which impressed my teacher.
I was pretty good at acting like someone else, but before
I could concentrate & become really fine, I noticed that
the only Indian on TV or in the movies was Jay
Silverheels, whose dialogue was not exactly inspiring. I
decided that, at least if I was a writer, I wouldn't have to
wait for anyone to call me before I could work. Today,
as a 47-year-old crank who will never get to be an
actress, I think about the nice Japanese couple on TV
who are advertising a bookcase system & realize that I
still don't see Indians on TV except to advertise trash
bags or to add ethnic color to white evening soaps
(which I watch just to see them). Of course, we didn't
even get that far until the last 10 years. I think about
Geronimo being played by Chuck Conners & about
Charlie Chan who was a white man. I know that no
Indian actress will be allowed to play Miss Marple,
which is no more absurd. There are no Indians alive on
daytime soaps, although for a while there was an "evil"
Asian woman, a schemer named Blair, who later came
back as a white woman. A miracle indeed, but soaps
are full of them. Black people are slightly more popular
than we are, though we'll never see a fine movie like
Daughters in the Dust on late night. I probably won't live
to see a time when schools won't have children painting

pictures of columbozo's boats "discovering" us. I'd be
really surprised if an Indian actress won an Oscar or
even played the lead in a movie where whites weren't
important at all. If Elizabeth Taylor & Claudette Colbert
can be Africans, why Meryl Streep could be Pocahontas.
Some people still wish we'd die off as quickly as
possible, as long as we leave behind all our good arts
& crafts. I've cried at hundreds of movies about white
people but I don't complain about it the way they do to
me when they read *Bury My Heart at Wounded Knee.*
Someplace in me, maybe in us, is closed over with grief
we have no words to speak. It's why we move so slowly.
This is not acting. Here we are. This is our land.
None of this makes any sense
does it?

for all Native actresses & actors

[41]

TINO VILLANUEVA

Scene from the Movie *GIANT*

What I have from 1956 is one instant at the Holiday
Theater, where a small dimension of a film, as in
A dream, became the feature of the whole. It
Comes toward the end . . . the café scene, which
Reels off a slow spread of light, a stark desire

To see itself once more, though there is, at times,
No joy in old time movies. It begins with the
Jingling of bells and the plainer truth of it:
That the front door to a roadside café opens and
Shuts as the Benedicts (Rock Hudson and Elizabeth

Taylor), their daughter Luz, and daughter-in-law
Juana and grandson Jordy, pass through it not
Unobserved. Nothing sweeps up into an actual act
Of kindness into the eyes of Sarge, who owns this
Joint and has it out for dark-eyed Juana, weary

Of too much longing that comes with rejection.
Juana, from barely inside the door, and Sarge,
Stout and unpleased from behind his counter, clash
Eye-to-eye, as time stands like heat. Silence is
Everywhere, acquiring the name of hatred and Juana

Cannot bear the dread—the dark-jowl gaze of Sarge
Against her skin. Suddenly: bells go off again.
By the quiet effort of walking, three Mexican-

Types step in, whom Sarge refuses to serve . . .
Those gestures of his, those looks that could kill

A heart you carry in memory for years. A scene from
The past has caught me in the act of living: even
To myself I cannot say except with worried phrases
Upon a paper, how I withstood arrogance in a gruff
Voice coming with the deep-dyed colors of the screen;

How in the beginning I experienced almost nothing to
Say and now wonder if I can ever live enough to tell
The after-tale. I remember this and I remember myself
Locked into a back-row seat—I am a thin, flickering,
Helpless light, local-looking, unthought of at fourteen.

JOSEPH LIKE

James Dean & the Pig

You can't just call it a pig,
    a friend tells me,
Pigs aren't just pigs.
They're boars, sows, gilts . . .
How can you tell the difference?
    I ask.
You can't unless you turn them over.

But James Dean, I think, is always James Dean.
Even here posed next to this gilt or boar.
In rubber boots with hook-&-ladder snaps,
grayish khakis & faded jean jacket, it's James Dean
leaning casual against the pig—
as if it were a prop in a photographer's
studio—& cocking his cap into the crook
of arm like an anointed king,
like Charles II in that painting:

    His horse beside him quieted
    by two small grooms. The hunt, far off
    in the valley, & the king
    stands high on the hill as if
    he's just stopped from the chase.
    Back home again in England,
    bringing French plays & baroque
    fashion—his brown wig flourishing down
    the satin blue of his jacket—his hat,

bristling with ostrich feathers, held loosely
on his arm. He supports himself on a silver

cane. And this is exactly how James Dean
is standing. In the center of the sty—
the dung & mud-splashed boards, by the windowless
door, he props himself against the pig.
His aunt's farm. New York & Hollywood
as far away as the continent will allow,
& his death in just one more year. But here
he is with an expression on his lips
that could turn into a grimace, a smile,
into an angry teenager dangling a cigarette
& posed kick-back against a red Chevy. Ready

to become anyone else but Jimmy Dean
from Gas City, from a long line
of farmers rising at 5 o'clock
& slopping the hogs. Jimmy Dean cruising
in a pickup Friday nights up & down Main Street.
Beside him a pretty girl, 16, nervous,
excited because she's heard he's wild,
he's alcoholic. She can't believe it—
he just needs someone to understand him.

In a gay bar there's a corner plastered
with posters—James Dean in a black overcoat
& slicked-back hair, ambling past New York's dawn
skyline. James Dean propping sharp-toed boots
on the buckboard's dash—a giant Stetson
pulled lazy over his face. His middle name:
Byron. *Fitting*, a friend says. And I find
it easy to believe, knowing a man
can keep a secret. Charles on his deathbed,
the restored Protestant king taking Sacrament.

Now here stands James Dean: hips tilted & thrust
slightly forward in an oh-so casual way.

[45]

This role he is ready to become
because he is the role. Jimmy Dean
stands somewhere in his father's fields,
waiting to take on this part,
this James Dean balanced against this gilt.

JACK MYERS

Mom Did Marilyn, Dad Did Fred

(handwritten annotations: "is" under "Marilyn"; "is" under "Fred"; "(Astaire)")

We sat there, her tiny audience,
as she slunk downstairs, poured
into her sparkling blue gown,
kissing the red-hot air and singing
"Diamonds are a girl's best friend"
into each of our little faces
that blushed at how deeply she was
committed to being sexy, and at Dad
suavely twirling her out the house
and down the street in his convertible.

(handwritten annotation: "Fred danced")

The tunafish sandwiches, the blitzed TV
faded in an obliterating glitter
of glitz and wet kisses, and I
with my face turned toward
the heaven of things I would do someday
made up my mind too soon
to have other notions of beauty.

(handwritten annotations: "for her (?)", "him", "Not")

SHARON OLDS

The Death of Marilyn Monroe

The ambulance men touched her cold
body, lifted it, heavy as iron,
onto the stretcher, tried to close the
mouth, closed the eyes, tied the
arms to the sides, moved a caught
strand of hair, as if it mattered,
saw the shape of her breasts, flattened by
gravity, under the sheet,
carried her, as if it were she, *(sexily) slowly?*
down the steps.

These men were never the same. They went out
afterwards, as they always did,
for a drink or two, but they could not meet *) thoughts of Guilt what were you looking at (naked MM) + what thinking*
each other's eyes.

　　　　　Their lives took
a turn—one had nightmares, strange
pains, impotence, depression. One did not
like his work, his wife looked
different, his kids. Even death
seemed different to him—a place where she
would be waiting,

and one found himself standing at night
in the doorway to a room of sleep, listening to a
woman breathing, just an ordinary
woman
breathing. *beauty is in life's breathe*

[48]

JUDY GRAHN

I have come to claim
Marilyn Monroe's body
for the sake of my own.
dig it up, hand it over,
cram it in this paper sack.
hubba. hubba. hubba.
look at those luscious
long brown bones, that wide and crusty
pelvis. ha Ha, oh she wanted so much to be serious

but she never stops smiling now.
Has she lost her mind?

Marilyn, be serious—they're taking
your picture, and they're taking the pictures
of eight young women in New York City
who murdered themselves for being pretty
by the same method as you, the very
next day, after you!
I have claimed their bodies too,
they smile up out of my paper sack
like brainless cinderellas.

the reporters are furious, they're asking
me questions
what right does a woman have
to Marilyn Monroe's body? and what
am I doing for lunch? They think I
mean to eat you. Their teeth are lurid
and they want to pose me, leaning

[49]

[handwritten marginalia: jealousy envy spiteful]

[handwritten marginalia: doesn't think much of pretty girls — + stupidity]

[handwritten marginalia: she was just a woman to + her beauty was what made her but she is still human]

on the shovel, nude. Dont squint.
But when one of the reporters comes too close
I beat him, bust his camera
with your long, smooth thigh
and with your lovely knucklebone
I break his eye.

Long ago you wanted to write poems;
Be serious, Marilyn
I am going to take you in this paper sack
around the world, and
write on it:—the poems of Marilyn Monroe—
Dedicated to all princes,
the male poets who were so sorry to see you go,
before they had a crack at you.
They wept for you, and also
they wanted to stuff you
while you still had a little meat left
in useful places;
but they were too slow.

Now I shall take them my paper sack
and we shall act out a poem together:
"How would you like to see Marilyn Monroe,
in action, smiling, and without her clothes?"
We shall wait long enough to see them make familiar faces
and then I shall beat them with your skull.
hubba. hubba. hubba. hubba. hubba.
Marilyn, be serious
Today I have come to claim your body for my own.

[handwritten marginalia:] She really wants to be sought after like MM was to have to beat off them

[handwritten:] because I got you!

[handwritten:] nudity, again!

LEO ROMERO

Marilyn Monroe Indian

Marilyn Monroe Indian
Luscious cactus
fruit lips
Tight sweater
and tight
black pants
She's got a movie star
look about her
Wind blows up
her dress
and everybody looks
Especially the women —— *really?!*
What's she got
that we ain't got
they whisper among
each other
White man approves
of such shapely legs
You're going out
on the town
to Manhattan's
and Los Angeles's
fanciest
You couldn't do
any better
than with

Marilyn Monroe Indian
by your side
Beautiful as she is
she can even read
palms
And no one doubts
her acting abilities
anymore
Me, she says modestly
How could all this
fame
come to me
Little girl
who grew up barefoot
on the reservation
By way of explaining her
other Indians say
She belongs
to the long lost
tribe
of albino Indians
out by Zuni
or someplace

SHERMAN ALEXIE

November 22, 1983

"we were doing laundry
when we heard it on the radio
& your father changed

the channel to some station
still playing music
& he asked me to dance
& we two-stepped

my heart beating
Dallas   Dallas
your father held me

against his thin chest
for twenty years whispering
'ain't no Indian loves Marilyn Monroe' "

CATHERINE BOWMAN

Jackie in Cambodia

The Air Force jet set down like a god
or a good Limoges teacup on the saucer
shaped plain of the Mekong Delta. She stepped
down from the craft all pointed foot etiquette
and creamy crepe suzettes, her blue serge
walk as marvelous as a White House sunset.
What a beautiful widow in a world
of widows! The name Khmer Rouge swirled
in her head like a new perfume. Half magician,
half princess, she was on a holy mission
with her knowledge of cultures and her pill
box hat medicine and heavenly wardrobe
from iceberg to tangelo she was still
Jacqueline to us, not quite Jackie O.

DENNIS COOPER

from "Some Adventures of John Kennedy, Jr."

In New York

It's hot, and smoggy as Mars outside
so he stops for an ice cream
in the nearest Wil Wright's
and the clientele goes apeshit.

A man who loved his father
gives him his place in line, next!
John asks for a double;
he gets eight scoops and a real smile.

Then he starts up the boulevard
turning every head.
A filthy breeze blows his Beatle
bangs straight back.
He's famous, even without them.

Now let's stay with a couple
John has passed by
and overhear their reaction.
But it's awestruck, clichéd,
and not worth remembering.

In School

When the professor tells his class
their homework is to write poems,
young John brings down his fist.
"But tonight the Knicks are playing Boston!"
He'll have to give his front rows away.

Instead he slogs through poets,
hates them all until William Carlos Williams.
"You mean this is poetry?" He leaps
on his notebook. "I can write this stuff
by the ton." And so he does, a twenty pager.

It's about his own brief life,
praise for the sports stars, shit for the press,
close shots at his deep dark family.
The next day he's graded on his reading;
John's poem is "I'm Going Nowhere":

"I never thought anyone died,
especially not me,
then my father and uncle got it from maniacs
and Ari kicked the bucket the hard way,
and I've started thinking of my own death,
when will it come and how,
by some madman out to end the Kennedys?
I hope so, and that it happens
before I have a chance to show my mediocrity.
I know that's clumsy rhythm
but what have I got to lose, man? . . ."

When John gets to these last words
tears shake his sullen reading.
Amazed, the professor looks straight
through John's tough punk texture,
and then an A+ flies John's way
like a fastball, or a perfect pass.

JIM ELLEDGE

The Man I Love and I
Have a Typical Evening the
Night Richard M. Nixon Dies

When he shuts the door against his day-to-day, "June, I'm home," the man I love yells as he does every evening at 7:27 sharp. He takes off his helmet and air tanks and hangs them on the hat tree. He sits his briefcase alongside it, on the parquet. He leaves his space suit on.

"I'm in the kitchen, Ward," I yell back to him. I take his supper-time favorite out of the oven to cool. My pumps clack against the linoleum floor, my strand of pearls glints once in April's fading light, and as I grab the tray and head into the family room, my skirt whirls in a perfect little circle just like those little ones ice skaters wear on TV.

He scratches the crane under its bill, pats the alligator atop its head, blows a kiss to the orangutan who blows another back. The man I love grabs it in midair and pretends to gobble it up—*snap!*—just like that.

"Are the girls home from obedience school yet, June?" he asks.

"Not yet, dear. Fecklar got detention for missing the litter box on purpose yesterday, remember? And Roxanne's out selling Tender Girl Scout Vittles door-to-door, remember?"

"Where did we go wrong with Fecklar?" he wonders aloud, shaking his head, rubbing his chin. Because he's only being rhetorical, I let it drop.

"Sit down. Put your feet up. Relax," I say. He does. "Have some milk and chocolate chips," I add quickly as I swing around on my heels.

[57]

The mountain of hors d'oeuvres remains stacked on the tray despite the law of centrifugal force.

"Did you have a good day at the launch pad?" I ask as the pot belly pig brings the man I love his slippers then the newspaper.

"A-OK," he smiles at last and rummages through to the sports section. "All systems go," he adds and gives me a thumbs-up.

After the girls come home, after meat loaf and potatoes au gratin, after we tuck the girls in and read them their favorite story of Spot scampering down hill and over dale then turn off the light, after Gracie gets into a jam and George gets her out, after Marshall Dillon rounds up some bad hombres as Miss Kitty beams, we slide open the French doors and slip onto the patio.

"Look, dear," the man I love says, pointing. Little more than a pinprick of light, Sputnik arcs through the sky. *Something that's travelling with a traveller*, we'll learn "sputnik" means during its twenty-one days orbiting. We don't know a thing about the Berlin Wall going up and coming down, or apartheid and Nelson Mandela, the Ozone layer or rain forests, John Wayne Gacy, the Menendez brothers, or Lorena Bobbitt. It's 1957, our first episode airs tonight, and the man I love hasn't even been born.

As if it were the satellite's wake, a cool breeze rustles my bouffant. I shiver once, just once, but the man I love puts his silver arms around my waist, pulls me against his silver chest, and suddenly, I'm all toasty inside.

PETER BALAKIAN

The End of the Reagan Era

Endless horizons of wheat and corn
out of Willa Cather's reach,
and Ross Perot moving through it all.

I clicked a lever for my candidate,
the curtains opened like at Oz,
and my vote blew out the doors of the Jehovah's Witness hall.

I walked back through the saffrony maple leaves
just wet enough to stick to my basement trap door,
and sat outside and read some student papers on the Gulf War.

I thought of the states floating in their electoral colors
on the screen the way the scuds and patriots
flickered in their matrix dots before and after

the Giants played the Bills on channel 4.
In another century Galileo said "but still, it moves"
under his breath, and today the Vatican agrees.

Since legends keep us sane, I think today
of Cianfa, one of the five thieves of Florence
who was clasped by a six foot lizard

who ate his nuts and went right up his torso
until the two of them were two-in-one.

I love the clemency of roads this time of year
the way they tail off to the beautiful barns.

WILLIAM TROWBRIDGE

Viet Kong

Each one showed me his gold medal,
talismans from F-b-i, a name too holy
for them to say. These agents wished
to trade questions for answers, something like
the cult of "Jeopardy." "Why do you spell it
with a 'K'?" they asked. I told them I knew
the state capitals but I did not know
spelling. I asked if I could try another
category, perhaps state capitals.
They said they believed I was being smart,
which is taboo, that I could remain silent.
I take this Fbi to be a jealous god,
full of paradoxes and taboos, but perhaps
not so good on state capitals.

A I

Blue Suede Shoes

A Fiction

1

Heliotrope sprouts from your shoes, brother,
their purplish color going Chianti
at the beginning of evening,
while you sit on the concrete step.
You curse, stand up, and come toward me.
In the lamplight, I see your eyes,
the zigzags of bright red in them.
"Bill's shot up," you say.
"Remember how he walked
on the balls of his feet like a dancer,
him, a boxer and so graceful
in his blue suede shoes?
Jesus, he coulda stayed home, Joe,
he coulda had the world by the guts,
but he gets gunned,
he gets strips of paper
tumbling out of his pockets like confetti."

Is Bea here? I say
and start for the house.
"No," you say. "This splits us, Joe.
You got money, education, friends.
You understand. I'm talking about family
and you ain't it.

The dock is my brother."
Lou, I say and step closer,
once I was fifteen, celestial.
Mom and Pop called me sweetheart
and I played the piano in the parlor
on Sunday afternoons.
There was ice cream.
Your girl wore a braid down the center of her back.
The sun had a face and it was mine.
You loved me, you sonofabitch, everybody did.
In 1923, you could count the golden boys on your fingers
and I was one of them. Me, Joe McCarthy.
I gave up music for Justice,
divorce, and small-time litigation.
And you moved here to Cleveland—
baseball, hard work, beer halls,
days fishing Lake Erie,
more money than a man like you
could ever earn on a farm
and still not enough.
Pop died in bed in his own house
because of my money.
Share, he always said, *you share*
what you have with your family
or you're nothing. You got nobody, boys.
Will you cut me off now
like you did
when I could have helped my nephew,
when you hated the way he hung on to me,
the way he listened when I talked
like I was a wise man? Wasn't I?
I could already see a faint red haze
on the horizon;
a diamond-headed hammer
slamming down on the White House;

a sickle cutting through the legs
of every man, woman, and child in America.
You know what people tell me today,
they say, *You whistle the tune, Joe,
and we'll dance.*
But my own brother sits it out.

2

A man gets bitter, Lou,
he gets so bitter
he could vomit himself up.
It happened to Bill.
He wasn't young anymore.
He knew he'd had it
that night last July
lying on a canvas of his own blood.
After a few months, he ran numbers
and he was good at it, but he was scared.
His last pickup
he stood outside the colored church
and heard voices
and he started to shake.
He thought he'd come all apart,
that he couldn't muscle it anymore,
and he skimmed cream for the first time—
$10s, $20s.

You say you would have died in his place,
but I don't believe it.
You couldn't give up your whore on Thursdays
and Bea the other nights of the week,
the little extra that comes in off the dock.
You know what I mean.
The boys start ticking—

they put their hands in the right place
and the mouse runs down the clock.
It makes you hot,
but I just itch
and when I itch, I want to smash something.
I want to condemn and condemn,
to see people squirm,
but other times,
I just go off in a dream—
I hear the Mills Brothers
singing in the background,
Up a lazy river,
then the fog clears
and I'm standing at Stalin's grave
and he's lying in an open box.
I get down on top of him
and stomp him,
till I puncture him
and this stink rises up.
I nearly black out,
but I keep stomping,
till I can smell fried trout, coffee.
And Truman's standing up above me
with his hand out
and I wake up always with the same thought:
the Reds are my enemies.
Every time I'm sitting at that big table in D.C.
and so-and-so's taking the Fifth,
or crying, or naming names,
I'm stomping his soul.
I can look inside you, Lou,
just like I do those sonsofbitches.
You got a hammer up your ass,
a sickle in between your percale sheets?
Threaten me, you red-hearted bastard. Come on.
I'll bring you to heel.

3

Yesterday Bill comes by the hotel
and he sits on the bed, but he can't relax.
Uncle, he says, and points at his feet,
all I ever wanted was this pair of blue suede shoes,
and he takes out a pawn ticket,
turns it over in his hand, then he gets up,
and at the door holds it out to me
and says, *You keep it*.

Today I go down to the pawnshop
and this is what I get back—a .38.
Bill didn't even protect himself.
You have to understand what happened to him,
in a country like this,
the chances he had.

Remember Dorothy and the Yellow Brick Road?
There's no pot of gold at the end,
but we keep walking that road,
red-white-and-blue ears of corn
steaming in our minds: America,
the only thing between us
and the Red Tide.
But some of us are straw—
we burn up like Bill in the dawn's early light.
He didn't deserve to live.
This morning, when I heard he was dead,
I didn't feel anything.
I stood looking out the window at the lake
and I thought for a moment
the whole Seventh Fleet was sailing away beneath me,
flags waving, men on deck,
shining like bars of gold,
and there, on the bow of the last ship,
Dorothy stood waving up at me.

As she passed slowly under my window,
I spit on her.
She just stared at me,
as if she didn't understand.
But she did.
She gave up the Emerald City
for a memory.
I'd never do that, never.
I'm an American.
I shall not want.
There's nothing that doesn't belong to me.

MAUREEN SEATON

A Story of Stonewall

June 27, 1969, NYC

A story of Stonewall goes like this: On the night of Judy Garland's funeral I was being raped by a man I'd met at Christmas in red velvet. It was something he would never remember, the kind of incident Judy would have endured in a haze of booze, ossified from the waist down, goofy the moment before, as if the bankruptcy rumors were all true. The amazing thing was his penis—tiny and senseless, it went in and out like a needle and what was I doing this whole time? *This is the end of my dreams,* I would have thought dramatically, and it was. After the hive of gays exploded on the city and, even though Judy was laid in state, I continued straight for nineteen years. Some men think she was special, misunderstood the way *they* were, all that dandruff you can say about a star who dies thin and fingered as a Kleenex. To me she will always be the leader of wind and slipper, the child who scraped jelly from a jar with a dull knife, a proud mustache of milk.

PETER GIZZI

Lonely Tylenol

There I could never be a boy
—Frank O'Hara

You have to begin somewhere.
The devil of your empty pocket moves as escargot
up the artery of a hollow arm,
ending on the lip of your dismay—it shows—
in the Brillo morning of a shaving mirror.
It is that morning always, and it is that morning
now, and now you must fight, not with fists
but with an eraser. The duelist awaits a ham sandwich
on the dock where your ship comes in.
Be warned and without ceremony take your place
as you have before. Only look once
at the idiot chagrin and smile as you ready your slingshot.
You are not alone in your palindrome.
Why is it so hard to know everything it said
when the mirror spoke. The book is darker
than night. Do you read me?
This is written somewhere and no one can
read it. It is not for them but to you,
it is a reproof from years of neglect.
There there. No place like home.

An Anointing

Boys have to slash their fingers to become brothers. Girls
trade their Kotex, me and Molly do in the mall's public facility.

Me and Molly never remember each other's birthdays. On pur-
pose. We don't like scores of any kind. We don't wear watches or
weigh ourselves.

Me and Molly have tasted beer. We drank our shampoo. We went
to the doctor together and lifted our specimen cups in a toast. We
didn't drink that stuff. We just gargled.

When me and Molly get the urge, we are careful to put it back
exactly as we found it. It looks untouched.

Between the two of us, me and Molly have 20/20 vision.

Me and Molly are in eighth grade for good. We like it there.
We adore the view. We looked both ways and decided not to cross
the street. Others who'd been to the other side didn't return. It was
a trap.

Me and Molly don't double date. We don't multiply anything. We
don't know our multiplication tables from a coffee table. We'll never
be decent waitresses, indecent ones maybe.

Me and Molly do not believe in going ape or going bananas or go-
ing Dutch. We go as who we are. We go as what we are.

Me and Molly have wiped each other's asses with ferns. Made emergency tampons of our fingers. Me and Molly make do with what we have.

Me and Molly are in love with wiping the blackboard with each other's hair. The chalk gives me and Molly an idea of what old age is like; it is dusty and makes us sneeze. We are allergic to it.

Me and Molly, that's M and M, melt in your mouth.

What are we doing in your mouth? Me and Molly bet you'll never guess. Not in a million years. We plan to be around that long. Together that long. Even if we must freeze the moment and treat the photograph like the real thing.

Me and Molly don't care what people think. We're just glad that they do.

Me and Molly lick the dew off the morning grasses but taste no honey till we lick each other's tongues.

We wear full maternity sails. We boat upon my broken water. The katabatic action begins, Molly down my canal binnacle first, her water breaking in me like an anointing.

DAVID LEHMAN

The Difference Between Pepsi and Coke

Can't swim; uses credit cards and pills to combat
    intolerable feelings of inadequacy;
Won't admit his dread of boredom, chief impulse behind
    numerous marital infidelities;
Looks fat in jeans, mouths clichés with confidence,
    breaks mother's plates in fights;
Buys when the market is too high, and panics during
    the inevitable descent;
Still, Pop can always tell the subtle difference
    between Pepsi and Coke,
Has defined the darkness of red at dawn, memorized
    the splash of poppies along
Deserted railway tracks, and opposed the war in Vietnam
    months before the students,
Years before the politicians and press; give him
    a minute with a road map
And he will solve the mystery of bloodshot eyes;
    transport him to mountaintop
And watch him calculate the heaviness and height
    of the local heavens;
Needs no prompting to give money to his kids; speaks
    French fluently, and tourist German;
Sings Schubert in the shower; plays pinball in Paris;
    knows the new maid steals, and forgives her.

MARTÍN ESPADA

Coca-Cola and Coco Frío

On his first visit to Puerto Rico,
island of family folklore,
the fat boy wandered
from table to table
with his mouth open.
At every table, some great-aunt
would steer him with cool spotted hands
to a glass of Coca-Cola.
One even sang to him, in all the English
she could remember, a Coca-Cola jingle
from the forties. He drank obediently, though
he was bored with this potion, familiar
from soda fountains in Brooklyn.

Then, at a roadside stand off the beach, the fat boy
opened his mouth to coco frío, a coconut
chilled, then scalped by a machete
so that a straw could inhale the clear milk.
The boy tilted the green shell overhead
and drooled coconut milk down his chin;
suddenly, Puerto Rico was not Coca-Cola
or Brooklyn, and neither was he.

For years afterward, the boy marveled at an island
where the people drank Coca-Cola
and sang jingles from World War II

in a language they did not speak,
while so many coconuts in the trees
sagged heavy with milk, swollen
and unsuckled.

CARLOS CUMPIÁN

No Deposit No Returns

While passing through a
pueblito en Mexico,
a koca-kola symbol
dominated the sky.
This koca-kola trade
marks the minds of many
who cannot escape the rape
of koca-kola colonialism.

Koca-kola CULTure has
captives worldwide,
filling factories with
alienated workers who'll send
a fresh supply of the bottled
caramel-colored sugar water
addiction drink to eager
mouths under the moon.

As people consume—Koke
helps prepare the world's
tomb.
Koca-Kola caca
has joined hands
with the ghost of
Huitzilopochtli
in carrying away our
teeth and rust.

Eso, koca-kola cabrones
have turned our bloodstreams
contaminated.
(Si, las aguas negras
del yanqui imperialismo . . .
la Chispa?)
"It's the real thing"
yes, it's conquered quite a lot
with lies, as it becomes litter
here, there, everywhere,
with its can and bottle shapes
refreshing the corporate elite's
bank accounts.

Who are those that push
this undernourished list
of drinkable ingredients,
leaving trails of lives
and bodies bent,
sacrificed for the
mythological progress
only Koca-capital brings.

O. F. DIAZ-DUQUE

Why Don't I?

for Mark who liked M&M's

It came one day like a thunderbolt,
charged by the sententious righteousness
of those who would have us damned
to the hell created by this new bug.

The numbness, the shock
was not so much that death at my door
might knock.
At a loss I found myself explaining
when,
where,
how,
and who might have given it to me.
Me! The one who knew the ins and outs
of that microscopic bastard
and its ghastly bite.

It's negative, she said, cheer up!
Worried well, that's all you are,
said the smiling woman patting my hand.
It's negative . . . It's negative . . .
But I sat dumbfounded, in shock,
and her words didn't register at all:
It's negative, isn't that wonderful
for you?

Come on, honey, let's go.
You look really bad, let's eat something, let's chat.
And picking me up by the hand,
my friend dragged me slowly from where I sat.
It's easy for you to say that I'm really all right.
See this spot? It's Kaposi's; it's the second time I've had it since March.

They died, you know, and I saw them.
One tried to sip a bit of water from my hand, but he couldn't,
and confessed to me that he was so tired, he couldn't even die.

And that other one, the kid from the farm?
I took him M&M's every night,
his only delight in this world of intravenous affection,
fag haters, syringes, and ignored cries.
But on this evening when I arrived,
M&M's in hand,
the nurse coldly said that he had died.

So, why am I here, tell me, why?
Just let me be, let me cry.
They were so young, those men,
when the virus got them,
and now they won't come back.

Why don't I have it,
tell me,
why?

JOHN YAU

Corpse and Mirror (III)

1

When the movie ends and the lights come on, the audience is puzzled by the sight of a corpse reclining on a velvet sofa in clothes of human hair. Each item has been carefully sewn, so that the hair resembles a white silk shirt and a three-piece wool suit flecked with gold.

On the mahogany table is a brass ashtray in the shape of a bulldog. Smoke curls from its nostrils as if it had swallowed a cigarette. An emerald butterfly glistens on his left index finger. In his bluish gray hands is a book whose pages are made of glass.

The next afternoon I drive to the outskirts of town, where there is a restaurant named after a traitor famous for his ingenious disguises. Many of its patrons think that even the name is a disguise and he still moves among us.

I have never been able to remember the plot of the movie, only the colors it traced against the arch of the bridge connecting the room's two halves together. On one side shines the movie and on the other sits the corpse. Passing back and forth between them is a conversation made of human hair.

2

When the movie ends, the lights come on. The audience is puzzled by the sight of a large oval mirror leaning awkwardly against a column, which wasn't there at the beginning of the evening's entertainment.

Scarves stop fluttering; and, one by one, hands settle nervously into laps, like birds circling the perimeters of their nests. Mouths twist beneath the receding wave of whispers, almost as if there were a place they could hide.

A reflection pierces the mirror, though the stage is empty. The men see a woman brushing her hair, while the women see a man trimming his beard.

Later, no one will be able to agree on what they saw. The memory of one event will twist around the memory of another. All that remains is the ache of trying to recall a moment, whose slanting roof of sunlight has long since fallen in. By then the mirror will have vanished and the movie will have started. This time in pieces.

KYOKO MORI

Barbie Says Math Is Hard

As a boy, I'd still have asked
why Jack must spend exactly
two dollars at the corner store.
Give him a coin purse is as
good an answer as five apples
and two oranges. Also: would
he bake the apples into pies
or cobblers, save the orange peel
in glass jars to spice up his
tea or cake? If his father
paints their house with Mr. Jones,
which man will take the peaks and
why? Would the raspberry beetles
swarm over wet paint? Why is
Mr. Jones slower than his
neighbor? If x equals y,
is it like putting apples into
cole slaw, the way a tomato
is really a fruit? None of my
dolls talked or grew hair. In
third grade, Satsuki and I
traded our Barbies' limbs so
mine could flex her left biceps
while hers sat cross-legged
raising one stiff arm
like a weapon. If Satsuki has

[80]

daughters, she might remember
the grasshoppers we caught,
how we cupped two hands together
into crooked globes to
hear them rattling inside like
a small motor. She would tell
her daughters: Yes, math was hard,
but not because we were girls.

DENISE DUHAMEL

Barbie's Molester

His penis rises before him, a compulsion. He would take hormones if he could. In his best dreams he is natural, purposeful, like a rising moon. He begged his parole officer: *please don't let me out again.* But the psychological report said he was ready enough.

His penis swells like a bump on the head and it hurts just as much as water on the knee. He's thrown away all his pornography and tries staying home as much as he can. He follows his counselor's advice: when the violence gets too much, he turns to another TV channel.

Things are tentative, though steady, until Christmas, when the Barbie commercials start to appear. He races to the toy store and yanks one of her from the shelf as hard as he can. When she doesn't struggle he mistakes this for love. Suddenly he's doing things even he's never thought of.

Wow — what a mind trip!!

Pshycn — I can't help it so keep me locked up

DANIEL MARK EPSTEIN

Mannequins

This indecent procession of the undead
   invades the Avenue windows, dressed to kill,
sporting tomorrow's clothes and yesterday's faces.

One struts in a velvet shaft of midnight blue,
     slashed down the back in a diamond heat of lust,
gold crown at the wrist and throat, a garnet ring.
Here Lucie Anne side-slits a terry dress
     trimmed in Venetian lace
and petal edging on the camisole. There a lady
    most unladylike, lounges
in silk of liquidly drapable muscadine,
    grinning the wine-red of wickedness. Another
borrows the schoolgirl's kiss, the cupie bow,
eyes round and empty as pots, and the apple cheek.
For we also yearn to join the innocent in their clothes:
    Jill in her jumper, Johnnie in his jeans,
sheep in their fleece, the pig in his narrow poke.

But I prefer them naked, the posturing frauds,
free from any trace of shame, and without nipples
    or the fur that friction-proofs our parts for love.
I like them headless, oh Marie Antoinette,
    what beauty knocked in the executioner's bucket!
I like them wigless, as a rack of bullets.
I like when a leg is kicked out of its socket
or an arm flings back in some preposterous gesture

[83]

as if to say
"So happy to have missed the agony of meeting you,"
or
"We who are early salute you from the backs of our heads." *Lahe!*
I love when the feet swivel for a fast retreat,
and the head jerks in wonder defying the neck.

But when they are assembled and decked out,
they turn vicious, whispering through the glass: —— *not the followers*
"How have you achieved your shabbiness? ——
Where is your glamour, the youth you were born with? *(face never ages —*
Where, if you have one eye, is the other, *hub (*
and if you have three limbs, where is the fourth? *of faces.*
Where is your hair, marcelled or carefully windblown, *of yesterday)*
your eyebrows, the artfully painted lips?
Put your face to the glass, you wretched snail,
kiss me, you desecration of a man."

saying
we — the people
are not reality
of beauty
+ fashion

Toys

[handwritten: what a complete change to old statues in the Vatican to toys]

Seeing them like this,
arranged according to size,
sectioned off by color,

I think it's not so much their being
made mostly for men, nor anything in
their being man-made; it's what

they are made of disturbs me: rubber
and urethane, plastic aiming for
the plastic of flesh,

[handwritten: the feel/look of!]

and just missing. Growing up, I was
told once that, somewhere in the Vatican,
there's a room still, where—

ordered and numbered, as if
awaiting recall—lie all the phalluses
of stone, granite, tufa, fine marble,

that were removed from pagan statues
for lacking what any leaf, it seems,
can provide: some decorum.

[handwritten: David covers himself]

I've never seen them, but their beauty,
I imagine, is twofold: what they're
made of, for one—what, in cracking,

[handwritten: fine lines of ancient wear + tear!]

[85]

suggests more than just the body that
came first, but the peril,
the vulnerability

that is all the flesh means to say,
singing; then, what even these
imitations before me—lesser somehow

but, to the eye and to touch, finally
more accurate, in being true
to an absurdity that is always there

in the real thing—even these seem
like wanting to tell about beauty,
that it also comes this way, in parts.

*are the
cracked
materials
more
real or
close to
real?*

torso??

bust

DAVID WOJAHN

My Father's Pornography

The semiotics not of sex but of concealment, the lessons,
    the legacy of dark.
It's a strongbox in the basement, a corner in his woodworking shop.
    Inside, a prostitute of
forty years ago is swallowing a massive, blue-veined cock.
    The man is wearing
boxer shorts around his knees, white socks. Another man,
    a black man, enters her

from behind. Her expression? Bogus pleasure, eyes
    histrionically wide.
The photographer, I suppose, is demanding she look horny.
    A few of the shots
are four-color glossy, most a grainy black and white. I've already
    said too much. What next?
The damp smell of the basement he so carefully paneled.
    No dialogue:

the father always silent as the men within these pages.
    How old is the boy when he finds them?
Twelve? Fifteen? Always the humid smell, his ears alert,
    waiting for the car-door slam,
the front door unlocking as his parents return from their
    Friday dinner out. Yes,
he is touching himself. The photographs. This is not how I meant
    to say it: start again.

In the bookstore, the shelves' collage of body and genital,
    stacked to the ceiling,
each book vacuum-sealed in plastic. From here across the room
    they're a sheaf of postage stamps
from some debt-plagued island dictatorship, its exports baseballs,
    wooden carvings, philatelic rarities,
And I am Baby Doc, my shades and leather coat, my kingdom
    Girls in Leather, American Erotica,

Hustler, Penthouse, Girls Who . . . The air
    conditioner, hissing.
Background music: big band songs. The curtained booths,
    my quarters. I would like it
to stop here. This should not be written down. Another poem.
    What could it contain?
A playlet. Empty stage and spotlight, my father lugging
    the strongbox from a corner.

Spotlight: my father in his hospital gown, the day before
    another week of electroshock.
If you look closely you will see him weeping, but I don't
    know how to tell you,
can't trust what I could say. I return to myself,
    and the curtained booth,
and the woman's face, crying too—the director no doubt
    goading her to grander

postures of orgasm, her blonde head thrashing, the film
    now wavering, flickering,
all the quarters gone. Then I'm paying for the magazines.
    On the car radio, white noise
of news and weather, Emperor Hirohito dying. He has not
    been told of his cancer.
Such knowledge, his doctors believe, will cause him
    too much fright. The Emperor has lost

a half-pint of blood, but today sipped a few spoonfuls of soup,
    his first solid food in weeks.

RITA DOVE

After Reading *Mickey in the Night Kitchen* for the Third Time Before Bed

I'm in the milk and the milk's in me! . . . I'm Mickey!

My daughter spreads her legs
to find her vagina:
hairless, this mistaken
bit of nomenclature
is what a stranger cannot touch
without her yelling. She demands
to see mine and momentarily
we're a lopsided star
among the spilled toys,
my prodigious scallops
exposed to her neat cameo.

And yet the same glazed
tunnel, layered sequences.
She is three; that makes this
innocent. *We're pink!*
she shrieks, and bounds off.

Every month she wants
to know where it hurts
and what the wrinkled string means
between my legs. *This is good blood*
I say, but that's wrong, too.
How to tell her that it's what makes us—

black mother, cream child.
That we're in the pink
and the pink's in us.

MAXINE CHERNOFF

Breasts

If I were French, I'd write
about breasts, structuralist treatments
of breasts, deconstructionist breasts,
Gertrude Stein's breasts in Père-Lachaise
under stately marble. Film noire breasts
no larger than olives, Edith Piaf's breasts
shadowed under a song, mad breasts raving
in the bird market on Sunday.
Tanguy breasts softening the landscape,
the politics of nipples (we're all equal).
A friend remembers nursing,
his twin a menacing blur. But wait,
we're in America, where breasts
were pointy until 1968. I once invented
a Busby Berkeley musical with naked women
underwater sitting at a counter
where David Bowie soda-jerked them
ice cream glaciers. It sounds so sexual
but had a Platonic airbrushed air.
Beckett calls them dugs, which makes me think
of potatoes, but who calls breasts potatoes?
Bolshoi dancers strap down their breasts
while practicing at the bar.
You guess they're thinking of sailing,
but probably it's bread, dinner,
and the *Igor Zlotik Show* (their

Phil Donahue). There's a photo of me
getting dressed where I'm surprised
by Paul and try to hide my breasts, and another
this year, posed on a pier, with my breasts
reflected in silver sunglasses. I blame
it on summer when flowers overcome gardens
and breasts point at the stars. Cats
have eight of them, and Colette tells
of a cat nursing its young while
being nursed by its mother. Imagine the scene
rendered human. And then there's the Russian
story about the woman . . . but wait,
they've turned the lights down, and Humphrey
Bogart is staring at Lauren Bacall's breasts
as if they might start speaking.

A Personal History of Hands

Spatulate is the word *Glamour Magazine* uses
for fingers like these, a sign
of *artistic genius and creative
inspiration.*

When I was 16 I knew I was ugly,
but I had beautiful hands.
The nails just grew into shape,
white moons rose out of soft pink beds
under a scattering of tiny stars
like the stars on the most beautiful apples.

For a while I was a hand model, let strangers
paint my nails flamingo pink and rose flambé,
deck me out in jewelry I would never wear
let alone afford. I had fantasies
of men who would love me just for my hands,
of the mother who had given me up
for adoption, seeing a picture
of my hands in a catalogue
and recognizing them as her own.

She'd be sorry. She'd look me up.
She'd be beautiful and kind.
A little lonely.
We'd see movies together.
We'd visit palm readers,

where we'd learn how to love
our hands for the way they unfold
into maps of what we're born with
and what we make for ourselves.

BRUCE BENNETT

The True Story of Snow White

Almost before the princess had grown cold
Upon the floor beside the bitten fruit,
The Queen gave orders to her men to shoot
The dwarfs, and thereby clinched her iron hold
Upon the state. Her mirror learned to lie,
And no one dared speak ill of her for fear
She might through her devices overhear.
So, in this manner, many years passed by,
And now today not even children weep
When someone whispers how, for her beauty's sake,
A child was harried once into a grove
And doomed, because her heart was full of love,
To lie forever in unlovely sleep
Which not a prince on earth has power to break.

OLGA BROUMAS

Rapunzel

A woman
who loves a woman
is forever young.
　　　—Anne Sexton

Climb
through my hair, climb in
to me, love

hovers here like a mother's wish.
You might have been, though you're not
my mother. You let loose like hair, like static
her stilled wish, relentless
in me and constant as
tropical growth.　Every hair

on my skin curled up, my spine
an enraptured circuit, a loop of memory, your first
private touch.　How many women
have yearned
for our lush perennial, found

themselves pregnant, and had
to subdue their heat, drown out their appetite
with pickles and harsh weeds.　How many
grew to confuse greed
with hunger, learned to grow thin on the bitter
root, the mandrake, on their sills.　*Old*

bitch, young
darling.   May those who speak them
choke on their words, their hunger freeze
in their veins like lard.
Less innocent

in my public youth
than you, less forbearing, I'll break the hush
of our cloistered garden, our harvest continuous
as a moan, the tilled bed luminous
with the future
yield.   Red

vows like tulips.   Rows
upon rows of kisses from all lips.

KATHARYN HOWD MACHAN

Hazel Tells LaVerne

last night
im cleanin out my
howard johnsons ladies room
when all of a sudden
up pops this frog
musta come from the sewer
swimmin aroun an tryin ta
climb up the sida the bowl
so i goes ta flushm down
but sohelpmegod he starts talkin
bout a golden ball
an how i can be a princess
me a princess
well my mouth drops
all the way to the floor
an he says
kiss me just kiss me
once on the nose
well i screams
ya little green pervert
an i hitsm with my mop
an has ta flush
the toilet down three times
me
a princess

PHILIP DACEY

Jack, Afterwards

It's difficult to say what it all meant.
The whole experience, in memory,
Seems like a story someone might invent
Who was both mad and congenitally cheery.
I have to remind myself, it happened to me.
The stalk's gone now, and Alma, the old cow;
And I fear only the dream with the shadow.

My mother had a lot to do with it.
In fact, you might say it was her beanstalk—
She scattered the seeds, I didn't, when she hit
My full hand and said all I was good for was talk.
She haunted me in those days: I couldn't walk
Anywhere without seeing her face,
Even on the crone in the giant's palace.

Throughout this whole time, my father was dead.
I think I must have felt his not-being-there
More than I would have his being-there. Instead
Of his snoring, his absence was everywhere.
So the old man with the beans, poor and threadbare
As he was, became the more important
To my boyish needs. Not to mention the giant.

Oddly enough, the beanstalk itself, which some
Might think the most wonderful part of all this,
Pales in time's perspective. Though my true home
Between the earth and sky, and though no less

Than magic, that stalk, in the last analysis,
Was but a means to an end. Yet, I must say,
I still recall the beanflowers' sweet bouquet.

Then there's the giant. What can be said? Nothing
And everything. Or this: if the truth be known
About someone so great, it was surprising
How vulnerable he seemed, and how alone.
Not that I wasn't frightened. I was, to the bone—
But it was his weakness, joined to such power,
I feared most, and fear now, any late hour.

The fruits of it all were gold, a hen, and a harp.
I wish I could say I miss my poverty,
When my appetite, if not my wit, was sharp,
But I don't. A little fat hasn't hurt me
Much. Still it's that strange harp's melody,
Beauty willing itself, not golden eggs,
Whose loss would leave me, I hope, one who begs.

Of everything, the strangest was to see
Alma the cow come back home at the end,
Her two horns wreathed in wild briony
And traveler's joy. Did the old man send
Her as a gift? She seemed, somehow, lightened.
I'd like to think I traded her away
To get her back, sea-changed, in such array.

So I sit here, my dying, blind mother
To tend to, and wonder how it was
I escaped, smiling, from such an adventure.
If events in those days conformed to laws,
I'd like to know—not least, nor only, because
What happened then still makes me ask, Why me?
Not even my mother knew, when she could see.

ROBIN BECKER

Peter Pan in North America

Mary Martin, leader of the Lost Boys,
when you flew across the stage in drag
in your tattered forest suit, teasing Hook,
some of us recognized you. Girl-boy, darling,
you refused to grow into any version
of manhood, while we cheered at the play

in New York, 1960, tomboys pulled from play
to put on dresses and sit among the feckless boys.
Years later, we cultivated our baby butch versions
of Peter before our mirrors. That day, we couldn't drag
ourselves from our seats. "You liked the play, darling?"
our knowing mothers asked. We dangled from the hook

of their question, the answer as overdetermined as Hook's
effeminate ways. Being a boy was best. Second best, we'd play
Peter in school plays, flirt with our Wendy Darlings,
and strap on toy sabers like pirates taking Lost Boys
hostage. After all, Mary Martin could fly, take a drag
from a pipe, dance with her shadow, reject predictable versions

of femaleness. Call it chutzpah or perversion,
we imagined ourselves: breasts bound, hooked
to guy wires, smartly dressed in roguish drag.
We took our own message from the play:
if grown-up, gendered roles awaited all girls and boys,
then woe to her whom he called "darling."

[101]

When the time came, we called each other "darling"
and fell into our own problematic diversions
and girl-girl relations. Next door the gay boys
camped it up, swishing around in capes like Hook.
Now we've got adult cult artists to play
the gender-bending game, we know the world needs drag

queens, he-shes, and transvestites at the drag
ball. Behind the hetero scrim, Mr. and Mrs. Darling,
fly erotic creatures of every sexual preference who play
havoc with your repressed aversions.
Skirt and slip, tank and tights, drop the baited hook
and we'll all bite—girls, boys,

everything in between. Drag revealed our own inversions
long before the Darlings were upstaged by Hook,
and grown-up play separated the Marys from the boys.

KRISTY NIELSEN

Self Portrait as Nancy Drew, Girl Sleuth

Sure there are some differences. I'm no virgin
for example, but I do know to apply
lipstick before jumping in my roadster.

Okay, Chevy Sprint. My mother
didn't die when I was young, but she
might as well have. And just like Nancy
I had a father who seemed more
like a boyfriend.

I have close friends, one butch, one femme.
Somehow I am distinct and better, smarter.
I am every woman-girl-child-teenager-
tomboy. You can bet I know how to protect

my treasure. Like Nancy, I find hidden doors
and passageways. Oh, the mysteries I have solved
with my second sight and keen sense of guilt!

I am fearless in my pursuit of truth, earnest
to a fault. When pushed into a corner
I say to the villain: I hope your motives are pure.
I will find out. I will expose you.

CHARLES H. WEBB

Rumpelstiltskin Convention

Little knows my royal dame
that Rumpelstiltskin is my name.

Circus Circus swarms with us: floors strewn
With straw, a spinning wheel in every room,
Gold lamé pouring from the slot machines.
Our name "makes us special," we say.
But no one calls us "dear Rumpy" or "sweet
Stiltskins." We don't marry—even each other;
Who worth having wants a Rumpelstiltskin?

At Caesar's Palace, Elvis imitators
Uh hu huh ecstatically. Long
John Silvers crutch across Treasure Island,
squawking duets with their African Grays.
Sir Isaacs juggle apples at the MGM,
And re-invent the calculus.
The Luxor writhes with Cleopatras
And their snakes until bedtime, when the royal
Headdress and papyrus skirt slide off,
And nude women shower as themselves.

We lose our nametags, but the name remains.
I drag mine with me like a dead Siamese twin,
Aching for the day—as the Queen teases,
"Is your name Doodad? Pepto Bismol?
Finiculi Finicula?"—I break, and scream,
"Rumpelstiltskin, bitch! You know it's Rumpelstiltskin!"

I'll throw her child, then, that I won fair and square—
The only thing that ever loved me—back
Into her pasty arms, and stamp so hard
One foot sinks deep into the dirt of this country
That "celebrates diversity." I'll grasp
The leg still free, and with one yank, tear
Myself like a wishbone limb from limb,
Thinking *Kevin*, thinking *Jimmy*, thinking *Bo*.

ADRIAN C. LOUIS

Sonny's Purple Heart

But it's too late to say you're sorry.
                              —The Zombies

I.

Man, if you're dead, why are you leading
me to drink after five sober years?
Sonny, can I get a witness?
I had a Snow White vision of the prodigal
son returning to America
that day of my final hangover.
I tried to clear the mixture
of cobwebs and shooting stars
from my brain with spit-warm
Budweiser, but the hair of the dog
just was not doing the trick.
I ended up pummeling myself
seven times that day and named each egg
white load for a Disney dwarf.
The first was Dopey.
The final Sleepy, I think, or Droopy.

II.

Last year you scrawled a letter to me
about your first and final visit
to the Vietnam Memorial and how your eyes
reflected off the shiny black stone

and shot back into your brain like guidons
unfurling the stench of cordite and the boy screams
of men whose souls evaporated
into morning mists over blue-green jungles.
You had to be there, you said.
That's where you caught the cancer, you said.

III.

Sonny. Tonight I had a dream of Mom's death
twenty years too late and now my eyes
will not close like I imagine the lid
on her cheap casket did.
I was not there when she died.
Home on leave from Basic Training,
you stood in for me
because I was running scared
through the drugged-out alleys of America,
hiding from those Asian shadows
that would finally ace you and now, now
in the dark victory of your Agent Orange cancer,
it gives me not one ounce of ease
to say fuck Nixon and Kissinger,
fuck all the armies of God and fuck me,
twenty years too late.

IV.

History is history and thank God for that.
When we were wise-ass American boys
in our fifth grade geography class,
we tittered over the prurient-sounding
waves of Lake Titicaca . . . *Titi* . . . *ca-ca*
and we never even had the slightest
clue that Che was camping out
en las montañas de Bolivia . . .

We never knew American chemists would
kill you slicker than slant-eyed bullets.

V.

Damn Sonny. Five sober years done squeaked
by like a silent fart and I'm on auto-pilot,
sitting in a bar hoisting suds with ghosts,
yours and my slowly evolving own.
When we were seventeen with fake I.D.'s,
we got into the Bucket of Blood
in Virginia City and slurped sloe gin fizzes
while the innocent jukebox blared
"She's Not There" by the Zombies.
Later that drunken night you puked purple
splotches onto my new, white Levis
and a short, few years into your future
this lost nation would award
you two purple hearts,
one of which your mother pressed
into my hand that bright day
we filed you under dry desert dirt.

THOMAS LUX

One Meat Ball

You gets no bread with
ONE MEAT BALL
ONE MEAT BALL
ONE MEAT BALL
said the song sung
by the singer
in the famous night club
with the revolving dance floor
atop a famous building
while I ate a steak,
or was it shellfish?
The waiter wore a tux,
the vest of which was stained by gravy.
The song's about a man
who has 15¢ (that's $2.00
in today's money) to eat.
He can afford one meat ball.
He'd like some bread with that.
The waiter in the song
says, with scorn, the above,
or, the singer of the song sings
the waiter saying this.
There's not much else in the song.
There often isn't in songs.
It repeats a lot: redundant
is refrain. The singer

is famous too, I'm told,
and rarely works a room this small,
famous but small. I like the singer,
she's got some pipes, but it's the song
I like the best. Outside,
through the huge banks of tall windows
curving into the ceiling: a million
and twelve stars; and across
and down in every direction: a million
and forty-two lights
of this great city,
in this late, very late, 20th century
in our United States: *You gets no bread with*
ONE MEAT BALL
ONE MEAT BALL
ONE MEAT BALL. . . .

AUDRE LORDE

The Day They
Eulogized Mahalia

The day they eulogized Mahalia
the echoes of her big voice stilled
and the mourners found her
singing out from their sisters' mouths
from their mothers' toughness
from the funky dust in the corners
of Sunday church pews
sweet and dry and simple
and that hated Sunday morning fussed-over feeling
the songs
singing out from their mothers' toughness
would never threaten the lord's retribution
anymore.

Now she was safe
acceptable   that big Mahalia
Chicago turned all out
to show her that they cared
but her eyes were closed
And although Mahalia loved our music
nobody sang her favorite song
and while we talked about
what a hard life she had known
and wasn't it too bad Sister Mahalia
didn't have it easier   earlier
SIX BLACK CHILDREN

BURNED TO DEATH IN A DAY CARE CENTER
on the South Side
kept in a condemned house
for lack of funds
firemen found their bodies
like huddled lumps of charcoal
with silent mouths wide open.

Small and without song
six Black children found a voice in flame
the day the city eulogized Mahalia.

JUAN FELIPE HERRERA

Iowa Blues Bar Spiritual

Little Tokyo bar—

ladies night, smoky gauze balcony, whispering. Tommy Becker,
makes up words to *La Bamba*—request by "Hard Jackson,"

mechanic on the left side of Paulie, Oldies dancer, glowing
with everything inside of her, shattered remembrances, healed

in lavender nail polish, the jagged finger nail tapping. So
play it hard above this floor, this velvet desert. I want

the Titian ochre yeast of winter, keyboard man, fix your eyes
on my eyes and tell me handsome, how long will I live?

How many double fisted desires, crushed letters, will I lift
in this terrain? And this rumbling sleeve, this ironed flint

of inquisitions and imaginary executors, where shall I strike,
what proud stones? Will this fauna open for me, ever, this fuzz

anointed beak inside the bartender's mirrors, etched doves,
a cautious spiral Harley tank, hissing, this Indian bead choker

on Rita's neck? How long shall we remain as wavy reflections,
imitators of our own jacket's frown? Who shall awaken first?

Margo Fitzer, the waitress? I will say, Queen Margo, sing to me
stoic priestess of slavering hearts, three faint lines creased

on your satin belly, toss our planet onto your umber lacquer tray,
too empty now; make the earth spin its dog rhapsody, erotic

through this silvery offramp and flake, unfurl. We tumble across
this raceway in honey glazed traces, our arms ahead, the hands

flying to Ricky's Ice cream parlour, outside. I want to own one
someday, maybe on Thirty Second Street. You will see me

in my gelled waved hair, my busy wrists—so fast, a clown's
resolute gloves, dipping faster than finger painting—except

I'd be stirring milk and the light chocolate foam of love, churning,
burning this sweet spirit, more uncertain, than the celestial

sheaths above the prairie frost. See the boy coming, they chide,
leaning, how he crosses his legs, his eyes dreaming, sideburns

just shaved clean. He weighs the sour slate on his father's breath;
perfume, fortune, cards left on the bleeding table. Milo Wilkens,
          drummer

at the curve, strokes his nipples with his arms as he hits the high hat.
Somewhere in the back rooms, I know, a shrine, orange sponge
          cushions,

two toilets and a wire wound wicker box, to leave flowers, occasional
offerings by the Johnson County dudes, detasslers in jersey ties.

Talk no more, enjoy. Darling singer, let your starry blouse sway me,
steal this fresh peach half from its amber juice; I want the moon

in this nectar, too. The flashing cymbals, feverish. Who can strike
a votive candle, love, or sleep in this electronic night? Just listen

to the two-part harmony, laughter, pealing beyond the cemetery,
          beyond
the Iowa river—where the spike hat rooster bristles his tiny ears,

bows his head and sips from the dark cannister under the carved
          pearlstone.
And then, returns. Let us drink, salute the bright spokes of meal,
          the dying

wands of river blossoms, grandmother's sacred hair; listen, her soprano
owl, her bluish melody, so thin. Another glass please, we shall dance

once again, our eyebrows smearing against each other's cheekbones,
        loud
with a Midwest sweat, a cantata from the cross-hatch amp, click it.

Click it, for wild kind rain, forgiving seasons, for the blushed bread
of our shoulders and thighs, this night, everyone is here. Even Jeff
        Yoder

came all the way from Illinois, to fill a bucket with passion, ruffled,
thick. O Sax player with a jail needle tattoo, leap onto this wet
        pavement,

call my lonesome tempest heart, its buried mother's kiss, bless us
in staccato, with quivers of Oak branch greenness and sparrow
        longings

riff over this brutal sky, give us your bell filled, conjure your topic,
our lover's breath. Blues bar dancers, jangling gold popcorn, chord
        makers,

opal-eyed Suzie in a flannel shirt; we beckon the spark, the flaring,
this lost body to live.

TIMOTHY LIU

Echoes

The world exists again. The roses drop their petals
from the railing of a ship and we wave goodbye.
An open hand is a hand letting go of flowers
in all their freshness, memory pressed into a diary
sinking to the bottom of the sea. All my life
the sound I've been trying to hear is the sound
of my own voice. I thirst in full view of the ocean
that lies before me. We are not swimmers, taciturn,
sipping tea without a twist of lemon. Outside,
the shadows in the orchard have merged into night.

                    *

I cannot help it, going on like this, the windows
turning colder by the hour. Once I was seduced
by the sibilance of tires in the rain while staring
into my coffee at a vacant diner. An oldie
on the jukebox made me cry, not words I never learned
but that voice which took me back to a summer flat
in Taipei, laundry sweating out of open windows.
I was two years old in a tub, Ah-poh singing,
her hands playful as porpoises. I would only cry
if Mother came to finish the job, tepid water
slapping all around as she scoured my genitals.
Whenever I hear a baby scream, I gag its mouth
to keep it quiet, just the way I want it.

*

When I turned seven, I made Ian lie down
on the bathroom floor, next to a crowded kitchen
where our mothers were rolling meat-filled
dumplings, dropping them into smoking grease.
I hummed a tune to calm him down, unzipping
his pants in order to rescue his penis
from a house on fire, that sole survivor we dressed
in strips of gauze. Later I felt the way you do
when spoiling a gift by unwrapping it too soon.
Still, I got what I wanted by taking on new roles—
a captain, a pirate, a preacher who promised
to forget the whole thing when it was over.
Only Cathy wouldn't shut up, even after I had run
my fingers over the flowers on her underpants
while pinning her down: *You're going to have a baby.*
Somebody had already dealt another hand
of bridge, each parent holding a fan of cards
with sailboats on them, when Cathy came out crying,
I'm going to have a baby, and to my relief,
all I heard was her voice drowning in their laughter.

*

I have heard that oldie blaring out from windows
of a passing car, from a beat-up radio lost
in a janitor's closet. There's this church
I would pass on my way to school but never enter.
It's like that, each of us minding our own business,
then one day we are called. Phone soliciting
was not my pick for a first job, but it opened doors:
*Hello. I'm with the San Jose Symphony. Subscribe
tonight and win a free cruise.* Over and over,
my adolescent echo down a reverse directory
until that voice: *Ever wanted a dick in your mouth?*

I've learned to say no, but then it was only yes,
yes to those lips moving across the face of the deep.

*

Sometimes it seems I cry for no reason, trying
to convince myself that I am still here. I draw
a square on my palm and say this is a prison
where we are born. Each day the walls grow more
transparent. The night of Jessye Norman's recital,
we stood up when she sang "He's Got the Whole World
in His Hands" for her final encore, our applause
shattering across the stage like glass roses,
her smile roaring through the hall as she sailed
into the wings, waving goodbye. It was over,
our voices released as if from an old Victrola
spinning on the ocean floor, each of us breathless
in that echo of the lives we have loved and lost.

JONATHAN HOLDEN

Liberace

It took generations to mature
this figure. Every day it
had to be caught sneaking off
to its piano lesson and beaten up.
Every day it came back
for more. It would have been
trampled underground, but
like a drop of mercury, it was
too slippery. Stamped on,
it would divide, squirt away
and gather somewhere else, it was
insoluble, it had nowhere to go.
All it could do was gather again,
a puddle in the desert, festering
until the water had gone punk, it
was no good for anything anymore.
It wears rubies on its fingers now.
Between its dimples, its leer is
fixed. Its cheeks are
chocked, its eyes twinkle. It
knows. Thank you, it breathes
with ointment in its voice,
Thank you very much.

J O Y   H A R J O

We Encounter Nat King Cole
as We Invent the Future

Camme and I listened to Nat King Cole and she sweetly lay her head
on the shoulder of some well-slicked man and off
she went some slow easy step some thirty years ago; it wasn't
yesterday but ghosts of time in tilted hats are ushered
by our heartbeats into the living room as we eat fried chicken,
drink Cokes and talk about swing, don't talk
about heartbreak but it's in the stirred air. How we loved,
and how we love. There is no end to it.
One song can be a crack-the-whip snapping everything
we were in the lifetime of a song back
into the tempest of dreams. And when the Cokes are gone,
chicken bones drying in the sun,
radio shifted into another plane of time, I don't know
what to believe. My heart's a steady tattoo of roses.
Camme and I go to sleep in our different houses, she without
her dancing man, and me with my imaginary lover
outlined in smoke, coming up the road. There's a song
that hasn't been written yet; the first notes
are a trio of muses in a songwriter's ear. That song will invent
my lover of evening light, of musky genius,
I know it. As sure as I know Nat King Cole wore white suede
shoes, and smelled like spice hair cream,
as sure as the monsoon rains come praising the dry Sonoran.
Yesterday I turned north on Greasewood
the long way home and was shocked to see a double rainbow

two-stepping across the valley. Suddenly
there were twin gods bending over to plant something like
themselves in the wet earth, a song
larger than all our cheap hopes, our small-town radios,
whipping everything back
into the geometry of dreams: became Nat King Cole
became the sultry blue moon became all
perfumed romantic strangers became Camme and me
became love
suddenly

MARILYN HACKER

Mythology

Penelope as a *garçon manqué*
weaves sonnets on a barstool among sailors,
tapping her iambs out on the brass rail. Ours
is not the high-school text. Persephone
a.k.a. Télémaque-who-tagged-along,
sleeps off her lunch on an Italian train
headed for Paris, while Ulysse-Maman
plugs into the Shirelles singing her song
("What Does a Girl Do?"). What *does* a girl do
but walk across the world, her kid in tow,
stopping at stations on the way, with friends
to tie her to the mast when she gets too
close to the edge? And when the voyage ends,
what does a girl do? Girl, that's up to you.

KATE RUSHIN

The Black Back-Ups

This is dedicated to Merry Clayton, Fontella Bass, Vonetta
Washington, Carolyn Franklin, Yolanda McCullough,
Carolyn Willis, Gwen Guthrie, Helaine Harris, and Darlene
Love. This is for all of the Black women who sang back-up for
Elvis Presley, John Denver, James Taylor, Lou Reed.
Etc. Etc. Etc.

I said Hey Babe
Take a Walk on the Wild Side
I said Hey Babe
Take a Walk on the Wild Side

And the colored girls say
Do dodo do do dodododo
Do dodo do do dodododo
Do dodo do do dodododo ooooo

This is for my Great-Grandmother Esther, my Grandmother
Addie, my grandmother called Sister, my Great-Aunt
Rachel, my Aunt Hilda, my Aunt Tine, my Aunt Breda,
my Aunt Gladys, my Aunt Helen, my Aunt Ellie,
my Cousin Barbara, my Cousin Dottie and my Great-Great-
Aunt Vene.

This is dedicated to all of the Black women riding on buses
and subways back and forth to the Main Line, Haddonfield,
Cherry Hill and Chevy Chase. This is for the women who
spend their summers in Rockport, Newport, Cape Cod and

Camden, Maine. This is for the women who open those
bundles of dirty laundry sent home from those ivy-covered
campuses.

My Great-Aunt Rachel worked for the Carters
Ever since I can remember
There was *The Boy*
Whose name I never knew
And there was *The Girl*
Whose name was Jane

Great-Aunt Rachel brought Jane's dresses for me to wear
Perfectly Good Clothes
And I should've been glad to get them
Perfectly Good Clothes
No matter they didn't fit quite right
Perfectly Good Clothes
Brought home in a brown paper bag
With an air of accomplishment and excitement
Perfectly Good Clothes
Which I hated

At school
In Ohio
I swear to Gawd
There was always somebody
Telling me that the only person
In their whole house
Who listened and understood them
Despite the money and the lessons
Was the housekeeper
And I knew it was true
But what was I supposed to say

I know it's true
I watch her getting off the train
Moving slowly toward the Country Squire

With her uniform in her shopping bag
And the closer she gets to the car
The more the two little kids jump and laugh
And even the dog is about to
Turn inside out
Because they just can't wait until she gets there
Edna Edna   Wonderful Edna

But Aunt Edna to me, or Gram, or Miz Johnson, or
Sister Johnson on Sundays

And the colored girls say
Do dodo do do dodododo
Do dodo do do dodododo
Do dodo do do dodododo ooooo

This is for Hattie McDaniels, Butterfly McQueen
Ethel Waters
Sapphire
Saphronia
Ruby Begonia
Aunt Jemima
Aunt Jemima on the Pancake Box
Aunt Jemima on the Pancake Box?
AuntJemimaonthepancakebox?
Ainchamamaonthepancakebox?
Ain't chure Mama on the pancake box?

Mama Mama
Get off that box
And come home to me
And my Mama leaps off that box
She swoops down in her nurse's cape
Which she wears on Sunday
And for Wednesday night prayer meeting
And she wipes my forehead
And she fans my face

And she makes me a cup of tea
And it don't do a thing for my real pain
Except she is my mama

Mama Mommy Mammy
Mam-mee Mam-mee
I'd Walk a Mill-yon Miles
For one of your smiles

This is for the Black Back-Ups
This is for my mama and your mama
My grandma and your grandma
This is for the thousand thousand Black Back-Ups

And the colored girls say
Do   dodo   do do   dododoodo
do   dodo
*   dodo*
*   do*
*   do*

JESSICA HAGEDORN

Motown / Smokey Robinson

hey girl, how long you been here?
did you come with yr daddy in 1959 on a second-class boat
cryin' all the while cuz you didn't want to leave the barrio
the girls back there who wore their hair loose
lotsa orange lipstick and movies on sundays
quiapo market in the morning, yr grandma chewin' red tobacco
roast pig? . . . yeah, and it tasted good . . .
hey girl, did you haveta live in stockton with yr daddy
and talk to old farmers who emigrated in 1941?
did yr daddy promise you to a fifty-eight-year-old bachelor
who stank of cigars . . . and did you
run away to san francisco / go to poly high / rat your hair /
hang around woolworth's / chinatown at three in the morning
go to the cow palace and catch SMOKEY ROBINSON
cry and scream at his gold jacket
Dance every friday night in the mission / go steady with ruben?
(yr daddy can't stand it cuz he's a spik)
and the sailors you dreamed of in manila with yellow hair
did they take you to the beach to ride the ferris wheel?
Life's never been so fine!
you and carmen harmonize "be my baby" by the ronettes
and 1965 you get laid at a party / carmen's house
and you get pregnant and ruben marries you
and you give up harmonizing . . .
hey girl, you sleep without dreams
and remember the barrios and how it's all the same:

manila / the mission / chinatown / east l.a. / harlem / fillmore st.
and you're gettin' kinda fat and smokey robinson's gettin' old

> *ooh baby baby baby*
> *ooh baby baby*
> *ooh . . .*

but he still looks good!!!

> *i love you*
> *i need you*
> *i need you*
> *i want you*
> *ooh ooh*
> *baby baby*
> *ooh*

GARY SOTO

Dizzy Girls in the Sixties

Back then even the good girls got dizzy
When you dropped an aspirin into a Coke,
Spoke with an English accent,
Or flickered a cut-out photo of Paul McCartney.
They got dizzy and dropped into your arms,
Brother said. And he said two guitar chords helped,
And the theme song to *Bonanza* made them walk
Backwards and wonder about the talent
That lay under a boy's black fingernails.
I played these chords. And when I could,
I shuffled my deck of cards and said,
"Let's get naked, *esa*. I won't tell—honest."
They didn't listen. Mostly they thumbed
Through magazines while teasing their hair
Into a nest of trouble. By seventh grade,
I was regrouping my hormones into one hard muscle
And no longer went around with my hands
Cupped in the hollow of my arms, the intentional farts
Cutting the classroom air.
It was a hit in fourth grade
But didn't work after the Beatles docked
In the hearts of girls and young mothers.
The aspirin didn't work either,
Or the English accent from a brown face
Or the chords on a Sears guitar.
I was nowhere, really, the cafeteria helper

Scooping chile beans into a plastic dish.
I was deeply troubled by high math
And such parables as the ark
And every beast in twos. One Saturday
I floated on an inner tube in a canal
And the best-looking girls at the end of our universe
Were on shore, peeling back
The wrappers of Butterfingers. Right there,
With sweetness greasing up their thighs,
I understood that I was too old to captain
An inner tube down a canal. I needed an ocean liner
On a sea splintered with sunlight,
Some stretch of watery romance. When I waved,
The girls barely looked
As I bobbed over the current.
The green cool water had shrunk my desire,
Thumb-long flesh just beginning to steer me wrong.

JAN-MITCHELL SHERRILL

Woodstock

That summer I went to Woodstock,
not for drugs or rock'n'roll; though
the constant rain was cleansing
and my wet jeans fit me like my soul,
I was there for Willy, to sleep with him
wrapped in the blanket I had brought
to cover us from home. I knew almost
nothing about him; what did I need to know?
A flat belly, tar-bright eyes, forearms
with one perfect crescent scar. I wanted him,
whatever name it meant I was.

I borrowed some drunk's truck
our last night there, drove us
plowing through fire flies so thick
in the heavy-lidded night we could
not tell them from the stars. We stopped
somewhere off the road, climbed onto
the hood of the truck while the moon
rose like a finger tip above us and
the radio crooned Otis Redding.
Slipping my hand beneath his shirt,
my fingers fanned to ultimate intrusion,
I touched him and we came across
the windshield of that truck,
our semen lit from the glow of the radio
inside, to sea foam phosphorescence,

lifeless, shining wreckage of old,
old treasure.

Far away from Baltimore that summer
we lay in the dark, a web of dew-wet body parts.
My sin was a sin of the eye; but I have grown
wide open, grinning pupil that swallows sight.
I want him back, that boy, touching
him and touching him in middle-aged sunlight.

PEDRO PIETRI

The First Rock and Roll Song of 1970

The unemployed sky above the clouds
that have replaced the hair on the buildings
Whose tenants live and look forward
to the last supper on the lost calendar
They swallowed years before they were born
and tormented by the consolidated edison grass
Who never took dancing lessons from the sun

The wind hits the clothing lines
secondhand underwear take off into eternity
The owner panics and jumps out the window
to look for them because he will not be able
To face his friends again if he gets buried
without those underwears he has not finished
Paying for yet. Last night a teenage mother

Put an airmail stamp on the forehead
of her illegitimate son and threw him out
The window to make it on his own in this
cruel world. The woman pleaded insane
To the authorities when she was arrested
and was sentenced to night school to finish
High School and become a full time waitress

When the war is over and the motion
picture industry shows how america won again
there will be nobody in the audience.
Little boys and girls shout at each other:

"My father's coffin makes your father's coffin
Look like a box of matches." The fee to pee
will be discontinued. Shaved head morticians

Dance with their favorite dead politicians
and the next president of the united states
Will learn how to read the help wanted ads

DAVID WOJAHN

"It's Only Rock and Roll but I Like It": The Fall of Saigon, 1975

The guttural stammer of the chopper blades
Raising arabesques of dust, tearing leaves
From the orange trees lining the Embassy compound:
One chopper left, and a CBS cameraman leans
From inside its door, exploiting the artful
Mayhem. Somewhere a radio blares the Stones,
"I like it, like it, yes indeed. . . . " Carts full
Of files blaze in the yard. Flak-jacketed marines
Gunpoint the crowd away. The overloaded chopper strains
And blunders from the roof. An ice-cream-suited
Saigonese drops his briefcase; both hands
Now cling to the airborne skis. The camera gets
It all: the marine leaning out the copter bay,
His fists beating time. Then the hands giving way.

MAUREEN SEATON

Blonde Ambition

The only miracle I ever wanted as a kid
was for my statue of Mary the Mother of God
to glow so I could feel enchanted.

I moved among grown-ups like a flame.
I was punctured by arrows of love,
I was boiled in consecrated oil, blameless

as risen Jesus, an anxious girl-child
of small radical expectations, sorry for sins
I'd never done. I stayed connected

to my he-lineage like a tiny fish
that lives on the benign whale shark
and follows him from ocean to ocean

in abiding complacency. Unlike *Colette.*
Or *Cher.* Now when I dream I'm flying
lonesome above other humans, striking

ballet poses and lifting off the floor
just enough so that they can't touch me,
I'm told I'm ambitious. Yet *Madonna*

scares me. I look at her peripherally
as if the radiance of her blonde ambition
is too bright or she might be contagious.

I'm told not to put her in a poem because
she will not endure the test of time,
she is no more deserving than Campbell's Soup

or the bee who gave his life when he
sank his pricker into my flesh. Meanwhile
I almost died on Friday at 5 on Half Day Road.

I used to tell my daughters not to worry,
no one dies until she's ready. For example:
My brakes gave out, I was closing in

on the windshield, the engine was moving
toward me like the will of God,
but I wasn't ready. I was totally alive

and dead at the same time. It was 1947.
I was about to be born, hovering
above two women strolling with sailors

in Elizabeth, New Jersey. One had the soul
of an angel. One the heart of a whore.
It was bright morning and the catbirds

were meowing in the old trees. The seaport
stank. I was waiting for someone more
immortal to stroll by, someone pregnant

with impossibilities. Is that a crime?
For example: You're allergic to bees.
The insect is heading toward your flesh

like a kamikaze pilot and kaboom
his essence is in your blood and driving
toward your vitals like a car with no brakes.

You: 1) Look around at your daughters
and memorize the exact radius of their eyes.
2) Examine your conscience and find it

spotless as your mother's kitchen floor.
3) Feel your death buzzing nuclear inside you,
fear lifting you up, cheeks hot with light.

PAMELA STEWART

Punk Pantoum

Tonight I'll walk the razor along your throat
You'll wear blood jewels and last week's ochre bruise
There's a new song out just for you and me
There's sawdust on the floor, and one dismembered horse

You'll wear blood jewels and last week's final bruise
I got three shirts from the hokey-man at dawn
There'll be sawdust on the floor and, ha, his dismembered
    horse:
Rust-stained fetlock, gristle, bone and hoof . . .

They'll look good hanging from the shirt I took at dawn.
Bitch, let's be proud to live at Eutaw Place
With rats, a severed fetlock, muscle, bone and hooves,
George will bring his snake and the skirt Divine threw out.

For now, I'm glad we live at Eutaw Place
Remember how we met at the Flower Mart last Spring?
George wore his snake and the hose Divine threw out—
Eating Sandoz oranges, we watched the ladies in their spats.

Remember how you burned your hair at the Flower Mart
    last May?
I put it out with Wes Jones' checkered pants,
The pulp of oranges and that old lady's hat—
I knew I loved you then, with your blistered face and
    tracks

That I disinfected with Wes Jones' filthy pants.
There's a new song out just for you and me
That says I'll always love you and your face. Let's make
    new tracks
Tonight, dragging the white-hot razor across our throats,
    and back . . .

PAULA GUNN ALLEN

Teaching Poetry at Votech High, Santa Fe, the Week John Lennon Was Shot

I

Crepe paper Christmas,
green and red, turns
and twists, symmetrical,
around the partitioned
segments of the barnsized room—
voices of brown and white young,
rejects from more hallowed halls
on their way to factories in some
nameless and partitioned open space
in the unbending world
of their faceless fate—blend with
mechanical and electronic chatter.
Noise everywhere, scrambling over
untouched books glossy and slick
with disuse. A groan and clatter
of highmigraine screech pulses
unidentified, predictable,
sets my teeth on edge.
My brainends turn, twist,
try to tune themselves
to unpredictability,
to something textured,

recognizable. Still,
I inhabit this slick universe:
hired to teach glossy poetry.
Through their eyes,
I see myself punitive, demanding, irrelevant.
Though I am not
vocationally authorized,
I hold the chalk.

Electronic mornings creep
over my horizon,
fill my days with danger, hang
ominous over the Rio Grande,
chase the mesas north.
On the highway early
driving north from Albuquerque
I saw sunrise gold and dayglopink billow
on the smoke of the electric plant
outside of Bernalillo.
So much beauty in the certain destruction
it spewed into the December crystal air.
Winter settling on the land, a nestling bird.
Stalks of winter-frosted grass
pointed to me my way, made
my pathway clear.
Last night on the late news
they announced John Lennon's murder,
said he died climbing the stairs.
Remembering when I
was on the other side of the desk,
the twenty years between,
I wept.
How had we come to this?
The shots that took him down
spewed a strawberry trail on the steps,

the blood washed away just after
by the city's rain.

II

The best of the world
slumps before me in the room—
minds that eighteen years ago
first turned earthward blinking:
oh yeah.
Wasted.
Turned off.
Tuned in to video narcosis,
stereophonic shuddering light,
in which, transfixed,
these naked angels burn golden pink,
their hopes and mine on dust and booze.
They smirk about "Ever Clear,"
explain when I ask
that it's 180 proof alcohol
unaware of the implications in the name,
of what
another time
the words might mean—
or perhaps not unaware.
There is a certain glint
on each institution-frosted face.
They have grown,
unawares, into electronic commodities,
haven't the will to fight
the mindless nothing that infuses
inexorable anguish into their lives.
Stoned like martyrs of their ancient faith
they go down their days
not understanding
how they've been crucified,

or by who,
they make do with plastic reveries sunk
in heedless desperation.
Synthetic clatter crusts
their days, makes electro-
chemical tissue of their gaze.

What world is this?
Cut off, torn away, shattered, maybe
they dream of when it will get better,
of when they will be free.

III

180 proof.
Neither womb nor honest texture provides
rough comfort or sure throbbing grasp.
Quivering, these desperados
hide beneath sham and sneer,
behind closed eyes, disheveled hair,
stoned on chemicals and beer.
What do they become, these children,
the same age as my own,
who I watch staggering into life,
despair rising
brown and stinking within their eyes
like poison on the desert air?
It billows gold and pink
around their faces, their helpless heads:
They do not plan, they do not dream.
There is no future they can bear.
I want to cradle them,
murmur to keep them from knowing
what I fear.
I will not let them see me weep.
I will fight with them instead,

sneer and rage.
Tell them to be quiet, to sit down.

IV

No munchkin voices. An English
sharpwood point breaks with a smug tap.
Muffled sounds rise in my ears,
the bite of lemon fills my nostrils.
They pass it around, juice sticking
to their hands. I am surrounded
by eyes that canny and closed
measure me, gaze surreptitiously
from faces no more than
nineteen years old.
Artificiality-induced
boredom barely masks
their scorn of the dusty
plastic tiempo their minds are frozen in;
barely differentiated into carpets,
chalkboards, partitions,
desks, shelves, jackets, slacks,
glossy animal posters on the walls.
They understand
the nature of their punishment.
They do not understand their crimes.
They sit behind plastic faces
barely differentiated into closed
and empty, resentful and dazed. They
are sick with disuse,
plasticized in atrophic rage.

V

Touch skin:
one's own

dewy with petrochemicals
soft for now.
Remember wood
gleaming and warm
accepting you—
smells and oils,
polishing.
Handle plastic
that refuses to recognize
whatever it is you are,
huddled into petrochemical clothing
acrylic
cold
unrewarding
no energy in it.
Know the exact dimension
of a dying soul.

VI

Tired.
Week nearly done.
Mind a tree,
peeling dead bark
littering the ground,
waiting
for the last molecule
to be released.
This rubble of ash
shaped into glazed and battered blocks
forms the walls, grey because they are
held together by despair.
Roughshod voices ride
the lockerlined metalclanging corridor.
Eyes glitter on the brink
of suicide.

The principal stalks the lateday halls
the tiny snackbar beyond the farther door.
He collars those who loiter
in these dispirited halls,
haranguing, ordering. His brown face
looks siempre tired.
His familiar Chicano body sags slightly
into his next word. He knows
what he sees. His limp loose tie
bespeaks discouragement, fatigue.
The students allow his harsh
ministrations, pretend to obey
until he is out of sight down the hall,
then return to loitering,
neck halfheartedly, play pinball
on a slightly sagging machine.
Two o'clock.
Ten more minutes and I'll be free.

I teach the students lost
to plastic rugs and desks,
watch silty minds
grainy to my touch's thought,
ooze helpless to the glazed acrylic floor.
Before me one young face
reflected in hand-held glass
gleams.

VII

Wood steel over emotional motivation sullen
firetaste smoke harsh hash herbs gross green
bitter lemonpeel coffeegrounds awful seeds
like wood burning nutcrust walnutskin goats
milk the aftertaste liquidy resin kumquats
sour cherries sharp a tar burn tongues fire

stream chill flight   harpoon   spiraling   tight
grapefruit tangy   bite spaced   torn from shoots
green apricots   sour blackberries   grogged air
kind of asleep   stomach hurt   chest sorry   full
tingle muscle   pulse   pulse   pulse   speed to
flight adrenalin spike taking off   meadows rise
in pleasuring thick as sour cream rancid cheese
fresh milk from fat dusty cows   taste of blood
coats warm throat what do we do with the hole
thats left   staggering   bleeding on the steps
ripe   ripped   on the powered air   stale burning
rising incense nicotine sweet   fingers nauseous
air content   powdered sugar hills   stiff grass
pointing billowing into blood   the pain   a mom
ent   only   gone fish   ride   lakes na'more clear
defined   strawberry place rising   a stair   plas
tic fields silent   time grows in cement cracks
soft fiber fall   a feather of breath   lemon air

VIII

Around me
the faces are forests
retreating into snow they
whisper about taking her down
giggle defiance . eyes
prepared for punishment
because they KNOW, in carnality
(¡oigan! ¡carnales!)
My words fall on history-reddened ears
She? / He? Who is it that speaks?
"See, man—I mean ma'am (smirk)
You know HE'S talking to HER
because the Beatles are male, man,
and HE says:
let me take you down"

(leering at the thought).
(Dying at the shot, yeah, man,
he's been taken down, *verdad*.)
They do not mention the tone of grief.

Winter here. We wish for spring.
For ease maybe somewhere
for running across fields
forever alive forever free
in some packaged plastic freeze-
dried recurrent fantasy.
But red with the ridicule of self-abuse
in front of me their postures are
vaguely fused to the carmine blaze of rage
that right to the quick bites deep,
touches me in that secret place
where no one dares to go, not even me,
though I KNOW
that inward lifelong sentence, that
single thought that holds
a life in matter's field,
that now bruised and icy bleeds
sweet juice red as ripe berries
on the forever frozen grass

IX

The noise and clutter
of each separate day
fuses into sound:
learned in grit
in multidecibel shriek, we
learned to say what there is to say
under bricks, under rubble of dead
elephants' dream
transformed into heaps of ivory

hedge against inflation
learned that daddy won't come home

he was never there anyway
to take it step by step
like one child stepped
(how many years ago)
trying to get home
scrambling among words
groping for comprehension
among the sneers alongside the tears,
cut off in the smoke of winter air—
a life and a not necessary death
sufficient for that time—still, quiet, dead.

Later that day it rained.

YUSEF KOMUNYAKAA

Never Land

I don't wish you were
    one of The Jackson Five
        tonight, only that you

were still inside yourself,
    unchanged by the vampire
        moonlight. So eager

to play The Other,
    did you forget Dracula
        was singled out

because of his dark hair
    & olive skin? After
        you became your cover,

tabloid headlines
    grafted your name
        to a blond boy's.

The personals bled
    through newsprint,
        across your face. Victor

Frankenstein knew we must love
    our inventions. Now, maybe
        skin will start to grow

over the lies & subtract
    everything that undermines
        nose & cheekbone.

You could tell us if
        loneliness is what
                makes the sparrow sing.

Michael, don't care
        what the makeup artist
                says, you know

your sperm will never
        reproduce that face
                in the oval mirror.

PATRICIA SPEARS JONES

The Birth of Rhythm and Blues

from the Billie Holiday Chronicles

Mid-February in America. Cold everywhere but Florida,
parts of California, and New Orleans, where Mardi Gras ends
in a gale of coconuts, trinkets, streamers and libations.

My daddy came back from the war, tall, slender, handsome.
Lonely in Korea, lonely in Arkansas. Lonely enough
to court my mother. Tall, pretty and tired
of her drunken husband, their store going bankrupt
and the grimy reality of small town daily life. A small town is
gossip and errands, work and more work. Schools closed in
   spring
(chopping cotton) and early fall (picking cotton),
the death-defying lives of all Black people—high yaller to
   coal black.
A Black woman's life is like double jeopardy.
All you win are dreams for your children
and the right amount of lies to make waking worthwhile.
Call it sweet talk from a colored soldier back from the snows
   of Korea.
Back from the nasty jokes, the threats, the fights in This Man's
   Army.
Back to America. Still alive.

Mama is early in her thirties. Promised so little and then
   hungry
for the world. For a world larger than the screen door that
   slams

early morning, and the reeking breath of a man once
   handsome and friendly and too easy with money. His
   money. Her time.
He's beginning to die.
Liver rotting away. He passes blood and thinks of a knife fight,
   some
juke joint when a Louis Jordan song blasted off the jukebox.
So fast, that song.
And funny too. Everybody shaking. Pelvic shaking.
But then a man's mouth opened, then another, and then
   slash—high cheekbones and graveyard eyes. Some niggers
   don't know when to shut up.
The red lightbulb shivers like sunset before a harvest moon.
My mother's husband singes the pain with whiskey. It burns
   the lining of his stomach. Starts the ulcer. Precipitates the
   cancer.
My mother's stomach grows and grows.
New moon. New hope.

My mother sings her own songs. Humming songs.
Something low into the earth
where the hurting stops and healing begins. That point where
   Billie hit
bottom and found the start of a global nightmare. Every
   walking man wounded again and again. Pierced in eye,
   belly, tongue, penis, anus, shoulder, foot. Bleeding and
   bleeding. All the walking men bleeding and bleeding into
   music's deep well. Quenching her joy. Clotting her dreams.
   Following her swaying hips screaming GIMME GIMME GIMME
Billie's at the corner where the dope man slinks. Willow in a
Harlem breeze. She strung out again. Big Irish cops, with
   nothing better to do, follow her. She's feeling evil. Starts
   her humming. They want to drink my Irish blood. They
   want that back. She's laughing low.

In New Orleans Professor Longhair has taken to the piano
and rumbled up a rhythm as steady as Saturday night loving.

[153]

And up North somewhere, someone is dreaming the Fender
    bass.
While across Texas, Black men in shiny tuxedos,
cotton shirts sticking to their skinny torsos,
rise and fall to the beat, the backbeat. A faster shuffle.
A wilder vamp. The beboppers are intellectual, you know,
and fast too. And everyone gets into the aviary act.
Flamingos, Orioles, rocking. Just waiting, just waiting
to grind you home.

Was it the teasing power of Big Boy Cruddup or Ruth Brown's
haughty insinuations or the crazy men in Macon with their
    too tight
suit pants and dicks as long as legend permits,
was it Aretha in the womb listening to Mahalia crooning
and Otis tossing footballs as the marching bands practiced
across the wide fields of the fifties South? Was it ever so
easy to make a voice that seduced and soothed as much as Etta
    James's,
who was pretty as Billie, and soon strung out too.
What made these people, Southern mostly, Black absolutely,
churn up rhythms rich as currents in the Atlantic?

Was it Billie standing in that pool of ugly light?
Fair skin wrinkling. Desperate for the ease of a needle.
Was it ever as sad as this? Not even the grave yet.
Eight more years before the coffin's fit to surround her.
And the men like hellcats cursing the click of her expensive
    heels.
Soft stone in her pocket. Rhinestones in her earlobes.
The dope man's leash shorter and shorter each time the world
    begged for more.

Billie shivers in her skin going slack. Joking the dope down.
Her face maps a bitter terrain.
From pain and back again.
While each door that opens for her closes.

But now, this moment, the door opens, a crack
where the light bleeds in, stays on her, merciless.

On the lonely roads in Arkansas, Mississippi, Tennessee
and Texas, skinny men in too tight pants shook out the blues.
And up in Chicago, someone with a harmonica wailed and
    wailed
I WANT YOUI WANT YOUI WANT YOU

and out of all the stars that fell on Alabama, Little Richard
    flipped
out of his melodrama and made this scream. His pomaded hair
flinging greasy love to the adoring girls giggling in the
    background.
While the men fingered each one of them.
Was it the first rape or the last smooth flight?
As the caped saxophone players and the gutbucket guitarists,
like the women with *Big* in front of their names—Mama,
    Maybelle—
relentless. Somewhere before the spotlight lengthened
to include so many, so beautiful, so always
rocking rocking rocking till the break of dawn.

Was it ever easy this motion of blood and mucus and dream?
First born and angry at the given world.
A noble operation from Caesar to a poor Black woman
already wanting to break this wall, as hand claps break a
    forest's
silence. Uterine wall collapsing,
so they cut my mother's belly and drag me,
wailing too.

ANGELA JACKSON

Billie in Silk

I have nothing to say to you, Billie Holiday.
You do not look at me when I try to speak to you.
You cannot look me in the eye. Your eyes
look elsewhere.
Your steamy mouth sewn up with red tears
is poised to speak
to someone.
The orchid in your hair grows, grows like
a spider turning herself inside out.
The shadow hangs
into your eye.

I have smiled the way you
do not smile.
I was just out of love,
and cold.
I was naked, beyond caring.
My smile, like yours, was a wry line
beside my steamy mouth.
My eyes, like yours, didn't look at me,
I only saw the fall
from
grace.

        (You lay down with music in the leaves.
        You wrapped him in leaves, in sheets.
        Your legs lindyed around him. Young

then old. Do not be deceived. The
thunder of the spider is no small
thing. You had your way with music,
and ate him. The memory hot
in your belly. Ours.)

You never want to let her leave.
She. The voice deceives.
You could hurt it.
It would kill you
too.
The dragline seeking
curving above Surprise.
Below
Just so.
Size is not the issue.
Volume not
the question. A hairline
fracture in the Silence
in which nothing rests.
The voice deceives.
Every thing
swings.

I have something to say to you, Billie Holiday.
Sew up your breathing, then send it back to me.
Fluent and ruminating the source of such anguish.

Look into my eyes.

If only it were not so lonely to be black and bruised
by an early-morning dream
that lifts the mouth to sing.

Here is an orchid, spideresque-petaled, glorious,
full of grace.

My mouth is on fire. Let it burn.

JAMES L. WHITE

Oshi

Oshi has a very large Buddha in him, one that can change the air into scented flowers. He used to be Tommy Whalen from Indianapolis but he had his eyes cut to look Japanese. He got started out in San Francisco in the early days when Buddha consciousness was just rising out there and people were still slipping pork in the seaweed soup.

At seventeen he did drag in a place called The Gay Deceiver and was billed as 'The Boy With The Face Like The Girl Next Door.' The owners paid him almost nothing and kept him strung out on hash in a little room above the bar, like a bad detective novel.

Somehow Oshi found the Zen community and started sitting za-zen. He collected 'mad money' from the state for being strung out. It's free out there if you're crazy enough. Oshi breathed hash and gin through the Buddha. Buddha breathed light and air through Oshi. It all changed his mind to indigo. Buddha consciousness rose in him until he didn't feel like the broken piano at the bar anymore.

Now thirty years later he has a permanent room at the bath house and prays for young boys. Doesn't sit anymore. Said he became realized ten years ago with a young hustler from Akron, Ohio who told him he could stop flying, just lay back and touch ground.

Old Oshi, very round now, jet black wig, looks like a retired Buddha in his cheap wash-and-wear kimonos. He's a graceful old gentleman Buddha. Buys everyone drinks. Gives away joints. Always high. Always lighting joss sticks. As he says, 'Giving things is just a way of getting on with everyone, you know, the universe and everything. It's like passing on the light.'

He told me once when he sang Billie Holiday's 'Blue Monday' at The Gay Deceiver they used an amber spot and he wore a strapless lamé gown, beaded his eyelashes, lacquered his nails, and the people cried.

BRUCE WEIGL

Homage to Elvis,
Homage to the Fathers

All night the pimp's cars slide past the burning mill
Where I've come back
To breathe the slag stink air of home.
Without words the gray workers trade shifts,
The serious drinkers fill the bar
To dull the steel
Ringing their brains.

As I remember, as I want it to be,
The buick was pastel, pale
In the light burning out of the city's dirty side
Where we lived out our life
Sentences in a company house.
Good people to love and fight, matters
Of the lucky heart that doesn't stop.

Beyond the mill street
Slag heaps loom up like dunes, almost beautiful.
Once we played our war games there
And a boy from the block ran screaming
He's here, it's him at the record store
And we slid down the sooty waste of the mill
And black and grimy we stood outside
Behind the screaming older sisters
And saw him, his hair puffed up and shiny, his gold
Bracelets catching light.

He changed us somehow; we cleaned up.
We spun his 45's in the basement,
Danced on the cool concrete and plastered
Our hair back like his and twisted
Our forbidden hips.
Across the alley our fathers died
Piece by piece among the blast furnace rumble.
They breathed the steel rifted air
As if it were good.

Unwelcome, I stand outside the mill gates
And watch the workers pass like ghosts.
I close my eyes and it all makes sense:
I believe I will live forever.
I believe the world will rip apart
From the inside
Of our next moment alive.

El Elvis

El Elvis
     puro pedo
          bien chingón

On a traffic light island
     on the corner of
          pobresa and maltrato

Hollering
     "NARANJAS BIEN DULCES!"
     at the insulated conquistadores del
          oro y plata

Con sus patillas largas
Como latigo quemante
Como pólbora en el aire bailando

El Elvis
     with his upper lip twitching
     but fingers too thick
     to play with guitar strings

Voice too rough to carry
     the high notes

Rust skin
     too dry & unpleasant
     for the mannequin dolls
     of pale soul rolling by

El Elvis
    de Mezcal Dreams
    & beer can nightmares
    De piramide ancestors
    & high-rise offsprings

"NARANJAS BIEN BIEN DULCE CABRONES!
Cinco pesos la bolsa. Aqui estoy
y no me voy."

MARY A. KONCEL

Come Back, Elvis,
Come Back to Holyoke

They still love you, Elvis. They want your hair, stories about your Harley ripping up pavement between Nashville and Memphis, your sequined gaze, your big-breasted women in too-tight bikinis. "Teacher," they ask me, "make us walk and talk like Elvis."

I tell them you're dead, fat, bloated, overweight and dead. But Juan Carlos insists that you live below him, that you stir steaming pots of black beans while singing "Maria Encantadora" on the radio every Tuesday. And Clarence calls you Father.

These boys need you, Elvis. Every day they sit, shaping their lips and grinding their hips beneath the desks. Across the room, I watch them, see little birds, baby roosters, dull voiced peacocks with bare chests and tender white throats.

Elvis, I'm only a woman. I can't do it all. I'm only a woman, and they're asking more questions. When I stand up, they point at me, stare at the split of my skirt, the breasts beneath the sheen of my blouse.

Next time, Elvis, forget the supermarkets in Denver, the trailer park in Lafayette. Come back to Holyoke. Teach these boys to be men, great manly men, men that love women, red meat, and '58 Buicks. Elvis, like the streets of Holyoke, my arms open to you, wait for you, your low lean rumble.

JANE CANDIA COLEMAN

Soap

The only time I ever watched *Dallas,*
JR was making out in a bathtub.

The choreography was superb.
Billows of bubbles hid all
the interesting parts,
and the faces—his and hers—
looked so bored I knew
it was a joke.

Deep in his heart JR was laughing
at us—idle women with nothing to do
but surrender.

CONNIE DEANOVICH

from *Ephemera Today* on *"All My Children"*

ONE DAY

Natalie gets discovered in her pit by an old, drunken transient wearing tweeds named Malcolm, to whom she tossed a $1,000 rope of pearls. He pawns them for a $200 bottle of cognac, and we assume he has fallen from a great height.

Hayley's hair is getting higher, like a hair-hopper of the early 60s, and I like it. She discovered that Natalie's near-twin sister Janet is impersonating Natalie, who she threw in the pit on her wedding day. The giveaway was that Hayley saw Janet dancing like a Frankenstein boxer to the heavy metal Natalie hates.

And that was it, except for a last bequest from an incestuous father and gross Craig moving away and Dixie, still with widow's tears, moving closer to new love.

ANOTHER DAY

Erica cuts her finger. Chuck questions Brooke about her possible marriage to Jack.
A new character, Dimitri, saves Natalie from the pit and brings her to a gothic castle.

Hayley and Brian take fingerprints.
Trevor goes on an undercover assignment—so inconvenient.
Janet as fake Natalie throws a fit at Jeremy.

Dimitri has flashbacks in black and white about a dead horsewoman. Mimi reluctantly gives Derek the brush-off while wearing civilian clothes. Helga the housekeeper makes soup.

MONDAY

Erica denies being the other woman because Dimitri's wife, Angelique, isn't a real wife, just a back-from-a-15-year-coma wife.

Sweet Stuart, Adam's "identical twin," is dating town misunderstood bimbo Gloria. The Club is aghast. Temporary character Red, the big strong redneck trucker, has been about to rape little, rich Dixie for many days, and now young stud Brian rides up on his white horse.

An-Li, who faked a pregnancy with blue food dye, begs Halley for forgiveness.

TUESDAY

Gloria's left town, fed up with being hated, telling Stuart she sold the painting he gave her and that it wasn't worth much. He believed the lie designed to turn his love to hate.

Dixie's left dead brother Will's apartment, guided by Brian who, for a young guy, is more wise than anyone. A rag doll went with her— a remnant of an impoverished childhood in Pigeon Hollow, a place name I always change in my mind to Pigeon Shit. Perhaps the producers wanted this association.

WEDNESDAY

Stuart stops Gloria at the airport and tells her he loves her and finds she really didn't sell his painting after all.

Opal tells "girlfriend" Erica Dimitri's a two-timer. Even though he *is* married, in name only, Erica is still in deep denial about being the other woman.

Brooke's love affair with Pulitzer-prize winning journalist Edmund Grey (where do they get their names?) is getting deeper, and Aunt Phoebe—our favorite character—is getting nicer. Every so often I suspect the dowager has the hots for her niece's new beau, but Phoebe, a pillar of the Pine Valley community, would never act on such low impulses. The lowest, after all, we ever saw her go was when they turned her into a white wine alcoholic. It used to be so funny when the Professor had to take her glasses away. She'd rave.

Another oldster, Helga, the housekeeping mother of Angelique, is on the warpath. She's determined to confirm her suspicions that Dimitri is sleeping with Erica.

Opal's suspicions that Dimitri may also be sleeping with his wife, Angelique, cause Erica to say "shut up," and to slam a door. She's always at her best when throwing a fit.

Forty minutes into the show, Helga breaks into Erica's house and Opal says, just before commercial, "Just where in the blue blazes do you think you're goin'?" After the break, Helga lies that the doorbell was broken. Who is she kidding?

Erica flies into Dimitri's arms.

A super mysterious black and white flashback of Helga's is the cliff-hanger. I suspect from it that Angelique and Edmund Grey—who seem at times to have the hots for each other—are really brother and sister.

THURSDAY

Most of the show was interrupted by Clinton announcing Gore as his running mate, but what we learn in 20 minutes is that Livia still loves Tom—she says, and that Dixie goes house hunting—bitterly.

Brooke hates a lot of things, she says on the StairMaster, and five of them're named Edmund. But, because of the interruption, we don't know *why*.

Flash! Dixie suddenly loves the idea of owning her own home and tells the frumpy middle-aged realtor not to call her Mrs. Lawson or Mrs. anything. Just, she says, call me Dixie, plain old Dixie Cooney. Ms!

The storylines begin to turn on revelations—whose brother is Edmund—and metamorphosis, as beautiful Ms. Dixie Cooney takes up the feminist lance!

FRIDAY

Adam thinks Erica is celibate.

Taylor, the new brat on the show, gets chewed out by Lucas, her stepdad and Terrence's suddenly unveiled dad. Terrence, who I just noticed is tattooed on his right shoulder, is back working at Tom's health club, where Brooke's been exercising for *two* days. What is she doing with her mouth? Is that supposed to be determination? Dimitri, the heir, and Edmund, the gardener's son, shake hands, but remain enemies.

Erica's no longer enemies with Adam because he gave her a divorce from their unconsummated marriage.

At the jeweler's, extra rich Erica and extra rich Dimitri bump into each other and arrange a night of sex.

Brooke, having exercised her anger out after two days on the StairMaster, tells Edmund she loves him, but he can't believe it because he still carries around memories of child abuse and believes himself unworthy of love.

Helga, I think, is carrying around a fake butt.

To set up a Friday cliffhanger then consummate another, a new character, Lucas's wife, arrives glamorously in Pine Valley, and Helga's black and white flashback is revealed: Edmund isn't Angelique's brother. He's Dimitri's brother—as if we didn't know.

MONDAY

Erica wears gold lamé.
Charlie returns with a new face.
Lucas's wife is named Vivien. She's very tres chic.

Edmund finds Dimitri in Edmund's childhood home that is now Dimitri's baronial hunting lodge—just as Erica is about to arrive for sex.

Vivien blew into town to discover that Lucas's skeleton in the closet is a long tall dark and handsome son.

Phoebe counsels Brooke on men and calls her "middle aged." Come on Phoebe, tell us what you really think.

Helga spies on Erica again.

Terrence returns to Livia's side.
Pregnant Opal eats right.
Ruth and Joe hug Charlie.

Erica and Dimitri have foreplay. We see her tongue dart into his ear—and hear it too. Is there a microphone in there?
Helga has a plan—no doubt to blackmail Dimitri.
Edmund proposes rashly to a startled Brooke.

TUESDAY—ALL STAR GAME DAY

Brooke spurns Edmund.
Edmund has tea with Phoebe.

Angelique and Jackson eat nostalgia at a drive-in.
Trevor buys an old house.

Brooke says "yes" to Edmund.

A sex offender enters—just his breath on the phone.

DANIEL HOFFMAN

In the Days of Rin-Tin-Tin

In the days of Rin-Tin-Tin
There was no such thing as sin,
No boymade mischief worth God's wrath
And the good dog dogged the badman's path.

In the nights, the deliquescent horn of Bix
Gave presentiments of the pleasures of sex;
In the Ostrich Walk we walked by twos—
Ja-da, jing-jing, what could we lose?

The Elders mastered The Market, Mah-jongg,
Readily admitted the Victorians wrong,
While Caligari hobbled with his stick and his ghoul
And overtook the Little Fellow on his way to school.

KLIPSCHUTZ

Funicello at 50

Annette has MS, she needs Mickey's help
out of the limo and onto the boulevard.
She has come to christen her star,
the one thousand nine hundred and ninetieth star
on Hollywood Boulevard.
She uses a walker to walk, but today
her hub takes an arm, her mouse takes an arm,
and she walks the Walk of Fame,
and stands over her star amidst all the hoopla
and thanks Walt Disney and cries and is thrilled.
Walt didn't make it—the dead are like that—
but Frankie showed up, and 300 fans.
Mouseketeers are forever, when TV was new.
MS causes cripples, like TV itself,
degenerative, still no cure.
Look. See the treasure chest, so many
would have died to pick the lock—
almost a separate self—
now indivisible, part of a whole grandmother,
well-stocked kitchen shelf.
The years, bursting with years. . .
The Vanished Dream glistens, intact,
a silo spills surplus youth,
and no war, no death bug to cull the boom crop,
under a full-bodied Southern Cal sun,
pre-implants, pre-sunblock, pink grapefruit

nipples, puppy love sand dollars starfish,
blown curfew skinny-dipping Redondo moonlight!
The Hymen Maneuver! Mythical sweethearts, waiting!
We never change, never change, never change,
as our friends age, landlocked and dull,
watching their newsmagazines,
tonight the domed man-made beach in Japan,
near where Mickey jobs out his watches
and they job them out again.
Put on your ears Annette.
Frankie, strip down to your shorts.
No more schoolbells, no more books. . .
On some far coast, the surf's up—

When I Think About America
Sometimes (I Think of Ralph Kramden)

raising that truncheon of an arm
to shake it, ham-handed and heavy
for what he was always about to say: *to the moon, Alice!*
in the dingy quarters

by the sea of human toil and information we called
The Honeymooners
on television in the fifties.

But why did we think it was so funny?
Alice was his wife and lover, and though it is hard, admittedly,
to picture their lovemaking—
the sweat he heaved into her with a fat man's
slog and fury, not

grace, don't call it grace,

until their headboard,
scrolled with grapes and angels in the old manner,
must have quaked like rails underground, years like that,
layered in concrete, deep,
absorbing the shock and just taking it
because someone said
Cleave Unto Him
and she cleaved, O she cleaved,
smirking—

I can't help it. I do.
Now my Sanitation-working neighbor with a
wife and kid and back rent hanging over their collective heads
like the ghost of Christmas future

fights solidly, drunkenly this week
for two impressive hours,
at the end of which time
they spill onto the matrimonial sidewalk,

dishing it out like this for love:

Leave goddamn you.
Leave.
Just take the baby seat and go. Leave.
I'm not your psychiatrist,
I can't help you with your problems and I'm sick
and you're sick
and I'm sick of you. Meanwhile

nothing in this scene is unequivocal.
The wife weeps and curses, throwing sucker punches.
The baby on the lawn
weeps and howls,
butting his head against a geranium.
And the baby's car seat, for god's sake,

lofted like the very torch of liberty itself
in the husband's arms,
to light the trees—then all of Bakman Avenue if he could.
A mighty conflagration to end
and start things
over again,

back before the high school prom ball spins too many mirrors
over their dopey, lovestruck heads;

before their nosey neighbor
(a stock character in these situation comedies)

puts her finger to the dial
and calls the cops.

*

Wait. Let me start again.
My father was a sociologist.
My mother a housewife stranded in the desert
without a canteen
if you take my meaning—

five babies in eleven years, very little money.

Not that happiness didn't exist for us sometimes
the way it did for the Petries
in black and white,
                Rob, Laura, their son,
Little-Pretty-What's-His-Name. No,
we had our moments,

our birthday parties and bocci on the lawn.
Our trip to Disneyland.
Our trip to Gettysburg.

But when Laura (Rob's due
home any minute. Quick, Milly, help . . .)
gave rise to a self-inflating life raft, huge, forbidden to her
   in her front hall closet
in New Rochelle,
in a place that was also a time and a lack, a pressing need,

we called it an *episode*.
We knew for her there would be
no real rancor,
and no fists raised

beyond the sweet vulgarity of working things out for laughs
until next week
on TV.

[177]

Or never.
Look, it's no one's fault; I can buy that.
Our noses flagged,
we were neither charming nor photogenic by the 1970s—
my prolix, super-unsubtle American family
pushing against itself like a live birth in the canal, cramped, uncertain,

angry, dropping down and down without a camera crew
or a script in sight.
What did Walter Cronkite say
when the war I grew up with
ended?
No end at the light of the tunnel?

Something like that.
And there wasn't a light or a life raft for years.

No wonder we'd long since
grown bored with television.
Petulant or high on sleazy
Moroccan hash, my brothers and I had spun from sitcom to soap opera,

from game show host to moon shot
to assassination
and back again, but O the moon shots!
Those men weren't heros; they were straight-arrow, uxorious types,
frolicking in their magic lunar vehicles
as though at some deluxe
country club—segregated, of course.
No wives or children allowed! And in that context

doesn't playing golf up there
make a lot of sense?
Low gravity, high density:

no need to plant our flag too deeply. Who'd want

to claim such a creepy place?
Let alone kill to breathe there.

        And the golf ball
hung like a word yet unspoken
for how many years?

     *

Don't look at me like that.
Violence, I have asked myself these questions
as a member of what family, what country,
what honor of blood to blame it on?

My father was a sociologist,
my mother an *agent provocateur* with a nervous habit of M&M peanuts
and staying up late all hours
in her splendid isolation,
for the purpose of taking notes, i.e., What
Jack Parr said.
Why Ed McMahon's teeth looked better
when he was wearing plaids,
why a certain starlet seemed despondent. Personally,

I was sleeping
vouchsafed in the heart of it all,
more abstract than any sleeping child.
Twenty-five years later,
I still can't find my face
in these two-way mirrors I've watched
like a burned out, brainlocked Saint Teresa, waiting for a sign.

     *

Here's a scene
from a movie I never saw on the all night
cable movie classics station:

           Barbara Stanwyck
      learning she's been framed, or at least suspicious,

reaches for a hankie but this time
gets a good idea, a hand grenade! instead. Catch this, she says.
America,
don't look at me like that.
The dust may never settle.

DENNIS COOPER

David Cassidy Then

David Cassidy picks me on the Dating Game.
I walk around the partition
and there he is. A quick kiss,
then Jim Lange gives us the good news.

"David, we'll be flying you and your date
to . . . Rio de Janeiro! You'll be
staying at the luxurious Rio Hilton
and attend a party in your honor!"

At the Hilton we knock the chaperone
out with a lamp, then we jive
around, smoke a little Colombian.
David says something to let me
know he's willing, and I get
to chew his clothes off.

He dances Swan Lake naked
and I sprawl out on the bed.
He saunters over scolding me in French,
and covers my face with his modest rear.

He gives me a few minutes
then he's up, blow-drying the drool
from his legs. He slips on a white jumpsuit,
runs a thumb across his teeth, and
turns to where I sit, still dreamy on the bed.

"Come on," he says, full of breath.
Never so proud, I bring my hands up,
rub his stink into my face like a lotion.
I will wear it to the party!

As the lobby doors open
reporters start the sea of lights.
The cameras take us kissing, dancing.
They angle to get David's sheathed body.
Girls watch his ass like a television screen
of men stepping onto the moon.

Little do they know what really lies there,
that this is no tan. "This is David,"
I say, smelling my face like a flower,
and pull him close, stoned out of my gourd.

T I M   D L U G O S

Gilligan's Island

The Professor and Ginger are standing in the space in front
of the Skipper's cabin. The Professor is wearing deck shoes,
brushed denim jeans, and a white shirt open at the throat.
Ginger is wearing spike heels, false eyelashes, and a white
satin kimono. The Professor looks at her with veiled lust
in his eyes. He raises an articulate eyebrow and addresses
her as Cio-Cio-San. Ginger blanches and falls on her knife.

*

Meanwhile it is raining in northern California. In a tiny
village on the coast, Rod Taylor and Tippi Hedren are totally
concerned. They realize that something terrible is happening.
Each has been savagely attacked by a wild songbird within
the last twenty-four hours. Outside their window thousands
of birds have gathered in anticipation of the famous school-
yard scene. Tippi Hedren is wearing a colorful lipstick.

*

Ginger stares back at the Professor. His sullen good looks
are the perfect foil for her radiant smile. The Skipper and
Gilligan come into sight. The Skipper has been chasing
Gilligan around the lagoon for a long time now. Gilligan
holds onto his hat in the stupid way he has of doing things
like that. The Professor's lips part in a sneer of perfect
contempt. Ginger bares her teeth, as if in appreciation.

*

Jackie Kennedy bares her teeth. Behind and above her, the muzzle of a high-powered rifle protrudes from a window. A little man is aiming at Jackie Kennedy's husband. The man is wearing bluejeans and a white T-shirt. There isn't a bird to be seen. As he squeezes the trigger, the little man mutters between clenched teeth, "Certs is a candy mint." The hands of Jackie Kennedy's husband jerk automatically toward his head.

*

The Professor is noticing Ginger's breasts. He thinks of the wife he left at home, who probably thinks he's dead. He thinks of his mother, and all of the women he has ever known. Mr. and Mrs. Howell are asleep in their hut, secure in their little lives as character actors. Ginger shifts her weight to the other foot. The intensity of the moment reminds the Professor of a Japanese city before the end of the war.

*

In his mind he goes down each aisle in his government class, focusing on each face, each body. He is lying on his bed with his white shirt off and his trousers open. Dorothy Kirsten's voice fills the room. He settles on a boy who sits two desks behind him. He begins to masturbate, his body moving in time with the sad music. At moments like these he feels farthest away. As he shoots, his lips part and he bares his teeth.

*

The Professor and Ginger are watching each other across the narrow space. The Skipper and Gilligan have disappeared down the beach. The Howells are quietly snoring. The Professor and Ginger are alone. From the woods comes the sound of strange birds. From the water comes a thick and eerie tropical silence. The famous conversation scene is about to start. Clouds appear in the sky, and it begins to snow.

[184]

JOSEPH LIKE

Postmodern: A Definition

Neither a lender nor a borrower be.
Do not forget, stay out of debt.
So the Captain on *Gilligan* sings
Polonius's advice to his son
who's really Mary Ann—another gender
mix-up, but still she's master-mistress
of her own passions.
Who knows about Shakespeare?

All this is sung to *Carmen*, of course.

But this play within the play of seven
stranded castaways never
gets around to the thing
that will capture the king.

No chekmate here.
No poison in the ear.
No tainted-tipped swords.

The corpses won't pile up
on this stage in a tropical jungle
where mild nights spin away,
and the moon, like some victrola needle,
carries the sounds of drums
and horns—*alarum!*
through the prop palms.

Where's the real play?

Maybe when the director takes on all
the roles—king and queen, lover
and murderer, mother and son, scholar
and mad man—he discovers
the beauty of flux. And this
is what causes him to leave
all the others behind.

GARY SOTO

TV in Black and White

In the mid-sixties
We were sentenced to watch
The rich on TV—Donna Reed
High-heeled in the kitchen,
Ozzie Nelson bending
In his eighth season, over golf.
While he swung, we hoed
Fields flagged with cotton
Because we understood a sock
Should have a foot,
A cuff a wrist,
And a cup was always
Smaller than the thirst.
When Donna turned
The steak and onions,
We turned grape trays
In a vineyard
That we worked like an abacus,
A row at a time.

And today the world
Still plots, unravels with
Piano lessons for this child,
Braces for that one—
Gin in the afternoon,
Ice from the bucket . . .
But if the electricity

Fails, in this town,
A storefront might
Be smashed, sacks may find
Hands, a whistle
Point the way.
And if someone steps out
With a black and white TV,
It's because we love you Donna,
We miss you Ozzie.

TV

All the preachers claimed it was Satan.
Now the first sets seem more venerable
Than Abraham or Williamsburg
Or the avant garde. Back then nothing,

Not even the bomb, had ever looked so new.
It seemed almost heretical watching it
When we visited relatives in the city,
Secretly delighting, but saying later,

After church, probably it would not last,
It would destroy things: standards
And the sacredness of words in books.
It was well into the age of color,

Korea and Little Rock long past,
Before anyone got one. Suddenly some
Of them in the next valley had one.
You would know them by their lights

Burning late at night, and the recentness
And distance of events entering their talk,
But not one in our valley; for a long time
No one had one, so when the first one

Arrived in the van from the furniture store
And the men had set the box on the lawn,
At first we stood back from it, circling it
As they raised its antenna and staked in

The guy-wires before taking it in the door,
And I seem to recall a kind of blue light
Flickering from inside and then a woman
Calling out that they had got it tuned in—

A little fuzzy, a ghost picture, but something
That would stay with us, the way we hurried
Down the dirt road, the stars, the silence,
Then everyone disappearing into the houses.

ALBERT GOLDBARTH

The Talk Show

> *. . . in 1930, The Bell Telephone Company commissioned one of
> their employees, Karl Jansky, to find out why the new car radios
> suffered from static. Jansky set up radio antennae, and heard a
> steady hiss coming from the direction of the Milky Way. Radio
> astronomy was born thirty years later.*
>
> —James Burke

A woman "heard angels." The paper says angels
sussurra'd her body, rang their praises daylong
through its reedy places, stirred her
smallest water. And elsewhere, Larry
"Dude Man" Chavez raises his #2 wrench
indifferently overhead on the C-track tightening line,
and feels something like lightning—only
there isn't lightning—beam to the wrench head,
branch down his arm, make all of his muscles
electric feathers, then exit his other arm out
its guttering candelabrum fingers and into
the frame of the Ford. It's stored

there. It happens. We all know it happens.
The cops and the hospital nightshift crew know
what a full moon means, and
if their decades of statistics don't cut diddlysquat
with you, here's someone being wheeled in
from a 3-car smashup while the universe hums
its lunar kazoo, and adrenalin everywhere dervishes.
And statistics on sunspots, and suicides.

And statistics on lines of magnetic pull,
and conception. We're the few but beautiful
units of the first day of the cosmos
densed-up over time; when the lady I love

flaps suddenly in sleep like a wire discharging, it
makes sense as much as anything—bad dreams,
zinged nerves—to simply say *we're* where
the Big Bang ripples to the limits of a continuous medium,
flickers a little, kicks. I've disappointed her
sometimes; and so, myself. I've left the house then,
while she slept, and while my neighbors slept, as if
I could walk noise out of myself
through darkness, finally dialing-in
the talk show where the blood calls with its question,
and the "sky," whatever that is, whatever portion we are
of it or once were, answers. And

I've walked past where the university's planetarium
dish-ear swivels hugely for the far
starcrackle Karl Jansky more primitively
dowsed. It happens any size; that woman? picked up
cop calls on her IUD, the paper adds, in bubble-bursting
glee. Although if angels are voices beyond us
in us, everyone's umbles are singing hosannahs
under their everyday wamble and gab. I've
slipped back into bed some nights and clasped her
till I slept, then woke to her heart
in my ear, that mysterious sound,
on earth as it is in heaven.

GALE RENÉE WALDEN

Misguided Angels

That summer the women sat on their porches
waving fans at cars passing.
A yellow Dodge Dart, the ugly pink Olds.
The boys in the street were playing
several things having to do with balls,
balls bouncing, rebounding, rolling
in the air, or on ground. Heat.
This was 1972 in the city.
The houses on our block were white.
On the television, the war, constant,
but outside on the street, a selfish joy.
None of these boys was going to go.

In the midst of old women on stoops
and children gliding through hydrant rivers,
what I hoped for was undefined.
That was the year each boy I touched
had smoothly veiled skin. Driving
from the city to prairies outside town,
we would sit on car hoods, a bottle of Blue Nun
between us, until the boy, silly with rock & roll
and small insincere punches, would
suddenly become reverent, look to the sky
and point out Orion,
unhinged sword hanging,
nipples posing as a shield.
It was foreplay for a kiss.

I thought it a tactic
learned at a secret school for boys,
an efficient segue between hormones & romance,
romance & hormones, the cosmos thrown in,
but I too would look to the stars, acquiesce.

*

Long after street lights came on
the men who thought America infallible,
like a President or a father,
stayed on porches smoking
and yelling for their long-haired sons
to come back home, lifting immigrant arms
to the warrior of night.

One man on our block I barely knew
came all the way back to my door
saying he was in a minefield and my face
had risen like a balloon.
He said this meant he loved me
and maybe I'd consent to be his bride.
I was fifteen and I didn't like the idea
of any part of me over there,
but he was shaking
and I had been taught to be kind;
I spoke of school and my boyfriend
who was Italian and jealous.
The man went away and for months
I'd see him from my window
limping up and down the block
until he started drugs and the limp
syncopated with a shuffle,
a kind of derelict two-step.

One night it was summer again
and we woke to trash cans banging
like timpanis, bouncing

off potholes and rolling down the street.
One by one little lights went on
like a village, and suddenly
everybody was all together again
watching him. He was luminous,
whatever drug he took was burning off
reflected in the dark, orange sky
and we cheered him silently,
cheered the visible damage done,
but when the men in uniforms
took him away,
he didn't say Vietnam
he said my name.

*

I awoke from a certain decade
tracing names in a black mirror.
The civil lines of the world warped
as the village expanded
to tangle names and faces—
betrayal no longer purely political
as the future unclaimed
walked a deserted street.
I married everyone,
as if that would help,
bride & grooms
we bravely marched down the aisle
to ungloried defeat.

Tonight in the desert
Orion hovers above
a constellation of memory
transformed into history
(lofty myth) changing
judgments & directions
until I am looking back, up, beyond

the Midwest, toward
a prairie of unscarred boys
who somehow already knew
what warriors we were destined
to become on our way to love.

WILLIAM CARPENTER

Ghosts

Every evening I do this. I stop work, and though
my body is longing for MacNeil and Lehrer, I change
into sweat clothes and into my Reeboks with their spot
of iridescent tape on each heel, so the runner won't be
taken for raccoon or porcupine; I run down Route One
to the suspension bridge over the Penobscot, as far as
the highest point, the center, two hundred feet over a river
luminous with ice or moonlight or a tanker's decklamps
or just darkness, which my eyes adjust to, till they can
see the small green light like a harbor buoy saying *jump,*
it would be easy, and I think, yes, this is a place that
could be right, this is a good time, before I forget what
I have seen; but I want to find out if Clinton is really
going to dump Lani Guinier, so I turn back, it's part of
my exercise, trying on death like an old suit from my
father's closet, then taking it off, hanging it gently up.
It's good for the heart. It's good for the bridge, too,
which loves to have someone perch on its guardrail, ready,
then decide to live. I pass the long riverside cliffs,
two miles without a house, no cars even in sight, I'm
running the yellow line right down the middle, full of
endorphin, WMJ in my headphones playing "Don't Be Cruel,"
which was the background music for my first ticket, ninety-
five miles an hour, and I think *Elvis, what happened,*
what did we do with all that time? I pull the headphones off.
I hear someone behind me—finally, a running companion—

and it's a friend, too, huffing and panting but definitely
keeping up: Dick Davis, who has been dead for eleven years
but he is now running beside me in the same shirt he had on
when he died. In the headlights of a semi I see he's shaved,
he's lost weight, and he's got a couple of guys with him, I
know them. The tall one was our conscience and our patrician;
tonight he's a mixture of moonlight and social justice.
The other's an old man, I can finally say it, and his feet, even
in this light, make the sound of slippers on linoleum.
                                                    I run
because my heart is vulnerable, because of the terrible things I
eat and think, I run so I can stop running and slip some rum and ice
into the blender and watch what happened to the world while I was
    out.
None of these guys should be here. They're out of shape, the wind
blows them off course. They're slowing down even now, they can't
stay with me, I'm out in the middle of the road again, running
the yellow line; they've gone transparent, you can see the moon
right through their pale elbows and knees. I can't hear them.
I put my headphones on and listen. Now it's Fats Domino:
"Walking to New Orleans." He's still ahead of me but I'm gaining.
I raise the volume. I quicken my pace a little, to catch up.

CAROL J. PIERMAN

The Apparition

> When the head of Jesus appeared on the bathroom door
> Nobody wanted to believe it, but there it was
> —Constance Urdang

One admires the American form of these sightings:
Jesus appearing on a grain bin or tortilla,
or, in one recent manifestation,
on a billboard in Atlanta, Ga.

Descriptions are so specific:
in Atlanta it's not just any old Lamb of God,
but Michelangelo's Jesus arranged artfully
among the spaghetti strands on a Pizza Hut billboard.

I can't help thinking how sacrilegious this sounds
(hair of pasta—marinara and mushrooms!)
though discovery moves discoverer unto tears;
it is a blessing which must be shared.

So the faithful tell of Elvis and Jim,
alive and still among us—browsing fresh produce
at a small grocery in rural Michigan,
prodding melons with a poet's knowledgeable touch.

I have examined the Jesuses of Michelangelo,
the soft-hipped hung ones of the drawings
and sketchbooks, the snake-haired pouty saviour
of the Last Judgement—beyond nebulous altar,

the abyss. So much agony and despair
mixed with the ghastly vindication of the saved—
it is a world of pain graced by the unexpected,
mystery surpassing inexplicable desire.

GERALD COSTANZO

Jeane Dixon's America

for Jim Crumley

San Francisco remains in grave personal
danger. Dubuque continues to be a source
of consternation for the entire Hawkeye
state. Tensions could diminish, though only
through an act of subterfuge.

New Jersey will be named in a paternity
suit, but will wage battle in open
court to preserve its good name.
Look for Minneapolis and St. Paul
to split, this time for good. Each
will agree they were never meant
to be together.

New York City will embark on a religious
pilgrimage, either to Rome or Jerusalem.
But there can be no forgiveness.
Overnight stardom is putting a great deal
of pressure on Missoula, Montana, which will
have to choose its roles carefully
in the coming months or risk
being a ghost town by the end of the decade.

Peoria must keep itself from overexposure
once again this year. If it succeeds, its
many problems will continue to go unnoticed.

Honolulu, weary of the long commute,
longs to be part of the mainland,
especially of southern California.
But with things the way they are now,
don't look for this to happen any time soon.

BLYTHE NOBLEMAN

Tabloid News

> Earthquakes could be caused
> by heated winds within the earth.
> First the lovely silence,
> then tumultuous convulsions
> shudder tectonic plates.

Instead of planting allium or amaryllis, the young woman finds herself
in the checkout line at the grocery store. Distant thunderheads signify
summer. She's buying apples and bread, nonessentials forgotten during
the regular weekly shopping. Her elbows rest against the cart while she
skims the *National Enquirer*: MOM FIGHTS TO KEEP HER CAT-
FACED BABY. Apparently she believes he could someday become
President, or the researcher who discovers a cure for cancer, cat-faced or
not. *Behold, I was shapen in inequity; and in sin did my mother conceive me.*

> Wind sheets surge with evening rain.
> Enlivened with moisture, seasonal bulbs
> boil up through the weathered crust.
> O the glorious peonies!

The young woman urges her cart through the narrow aisle. Lo, the
scents of contentment: waxed apple, cured yeast, bleached linoleum.
Familiar extracts of peppermint and chocolate tempt from the shelf
beside her. Sodium vapor lights conjure illusions of overcast, lifting
the shadows from her face, paling delicious apples, curly endive, mis-
shapen cauliflower, of all their earthly splendor. Even the sour oranges
appear to be otherworldly. FAMILY LIVES ON PET FOOD AND

LOVES IT. *Yea, take the sacrament of the Lord's supper. Body of Christ transgress our sins.*

> Burgeoning dwarf tulip.
> Blooming yellow narcissus.
> Their petals are edible.
> Each night she feels the ceiling weep
> with mercurified rain. Droplets
> slide from the roof like loose change.

Grasping her elbow, a strange woman accosts her in the checkout line. *What kind of outfit is that for a Sunday? I've had both my breasts removed. They're still beautiful. Would you like to see them?* The breastless woman raises her blouse, her milk-white skin smooth as a neonate. How could she apologize? The resin of tar and sugary bourbon bind the limited breadth between them. The checkout girl drags bar codes over the laser light. The young woman reads: BIGFOOT GOES ON RAMPAGE. You can see deep grey skin beneath his wooly pelt, yellow fangs like a mountain lion's. *There is no remembrance of former things: neither shall there be any remembrance of things that are to come with those that shall come after.*

> Faithful to the beneficence
> of well drained soil,
> abundance of sun,
> Dutch irises proliferate at last,
> holding out until wriggling pistil and stamen
> propel them past the lofty hyacinths,
> beyond the most brilliant blue.

Paper or plastic? the bag boy asks, *Paper or plastic?* The young woman pays for her apples and bread. MUSIC THAT CAN CURE DISEASE. The voices of Bing Crosby and Frank Sinatra are highly effective against cancer. Tom Jones relieves depression. Conway Twitty and Loretta Lynn cure sinus problems. *Vanity of vanities; all is vanity.*

> The apples will feel so cold
> against her teeth.
> The bread on her tongue

will taste like salted cotton.
Daffodils ascend the humid topsoil.
Crocuses close at dusk.
The coins in her purse
clamor like a carillon.

ALLEN GINSBERG

A Supermarket in California

What thoughts I have of you tonight, Walt Whitman, for I walked down the sidestreets under the trees with a headache self-conscious looking at the full moon.

In my hungry fatigue, and shopping for images, I went into the neon fruit supermarket, dreaming of your enumerations!

What peaches and what penumbras! Whole families shopping at night! Aisles full of husbands! Wives in the avocados, babies in the tomatoes!—and you, García Lorca, what were you doing down by the watermelons?

I saw you, Walt Whitman, childless, lonely old grubber, poking among the meats in the refrigerator and eyeing the grocery boys.

I heard you asking questions of each: Who killed the pork chops? What price bananas? Are you my Angel?

I wandered in and out of the brilliant stacks of cans following you, and followed in my imagination by the store detective.

We strode down the open corridors together in our solitary fancy tasting artichokes, possessing every frozen delicacy, and never passing the cashier.

Where are we going, Walt Whitman? The doors close in an hour. Which way does your beard point tonight?

(I touch your book and dream of our odyssey in the supermarket and feel absurd.)

Will we walk all night through solitary streets? The trees add shade to shade, lights out in the houses, we'll both be lonely.

Will we stroll dreaming of the lost America of love past blue automobiles in driveways, home to our silent cottage?

Ah, dear father, graybeard, lonely old courage-teacher, what America did you have when Charon quit poling his ferry and you got out on a smoking bank and stood watching the boat disappear on the black waters of Lethe?

Berkeley 1955

G. E. MURRAY

Shopping for Midnight

There you go, it's everywhere
here, waiting for me at ridiculous prices,
   the essential mood—collected
and perfect-bound—hidden, certainly,
     like the best of bargains,
among tampons & pickles & paperwares,
   down these aisles I tour at midnight.

     A browser at heart,
I carry no money. It's safer that way,
   as the average retail clerk
will ply me with replicas, expensive
     imitations of my prize.
And I have been taken for an easy target
   before, buying dreams of blood

     and summer at discount.
Once, guilty of wearing an oversized coat
   to market, a thief, I resisted
the sweet commerce of a career angel,
     boosting her instead
of her temporary goods. But shopping
   for the darkest of bones demands nerve,

     a special setting, instinct.
There are, naturally, no rules of search
   or purchase; no adequate samples.
Not necessary. The time will arrive when

I round a corner perfectly
and find it, waiting like a mouse, enormous
    as Canada, the perennial top-shelf item.

    It belongs somewhere, and only
there, mine to find alone, marked down
    like contaminated vegetables,
a fish found breathing on the beach, harvest
        of any old night, dampish,
twisted, leaving me to decide whether
    to steal, borrow, or merely adore it.

JIM ELLEDGE

The Man I Love and I Shop at Jewel

Untouched, the door swings open before us, and—*voilà!*—we're in the produce section. We pass up the bananas and zucchini, but can't resist squeezing hot-house tomatoes, knock-knock joking with the cantaloupe. He breaks a bulb of garlic into cloves, then snaps one clove open and rubs it behind his ear. I grow dizzy, lay my head on the produce scale, and growl.

We ignore the stares of the biker chicks and the grandmas pushing carts, the retired high-school coaches and fundamentalist preachers lugging baskets.

Aisle 2: Cellophane crackles as we pass. Aisle 3: Pop tops snap open, spew. Down the paper products aisle, boxes of Reynolds Wrap and packages of Charmin split open, unroll, festoon themselves across the ceiling.

"Stay close," I say.
He says, "StaSof."
"Huggies," he says.
I say, "Depends."

Theft detection cameras spin planet-like on their pivots.

"Fluorescence," I say.
He says, "Flower essence."

For hours we plunder the shelves and, aisles later, change our minds and return some of the loot. Our peg legs tap 50s lyrics in Morse Code on the glistening tiles, counterpoint the piped-in Muzak, our vision narrowed string-straight by patched eyes, our hooks perfectly adept at snagging our hearts' tamper-proof treasures.

Then, as we pull into the 10-items-or-less check-out bay, I lose control, climb onto the conveyor belt, hang ten to Don Ho's greatest hit past the *Enquirer* and *Weekly World Report*, pipe-line through the miseries of talk-show hosts and soap-opera stars, of Liz and Magic, of Di and the Kennedys as crowds form: the Morton Salt girl hand-to-fin with Charlie the Tuna; Aunt Jemima, Sara Lee, and Mrs. Butterworth closely flanking a blushing Oscar Mayer, their hands moving unfettered, wildly, and out of sight—and that cereal's toucan.

Blowing kisses to my fans, I squeal, *This* is *life*, in my best Richard Simmons, as the man I love pays the cashier what the cash register says we owe and snags the "Paper-or-plastic?" the bagger offers. Waving bye-bye to the crowds, *This* is *what it's all about*, I grunt in my best Steve Reeves.

Then, as the door opens all by itself again and we return into the arms of the universe, I belt out "I feel pretty, oh, so pretty" in the best Ethel Merman I can muster.

Mail Order Catalogs

Pewter loons, ceramic bunnies, and faux bamboo
are for the suburbs, and bird feeders in Tudor
and saltbox models, and tulips to force in delft.

But in smoky bars in small towns late on week nights,
where the old songs on the jukebox call in
their emotional debts only from habit,

for everyone's derisively broke, and farther out
in the washes and hollows from which men
drive vehicles to town to apply for loans for vehicles,

and from which women must buy a good dress by mail—
loneliness is the product and the customer gets sold to it:
country music, booze, and sunset shot through the cheesecloth

of topsoil powdered as fine in the dusky air as make-up
rich women wear back east. Once this darkening sky
was ocean thousands of feet up, and we were floor.

NAOMI SHIHAB NYE

Catalogue Army

Something has happened to my name.
It now appears on catalogues
for towels and hiking equipment,
dresses spun in India,
hand-colored prints of parrots and eggs.
Fifty tulips are on their way
if I will open the door.
Dishrags from North Carolina
unstack themselves in the Smoky Mountains
and make a beeline for my sink.

I write a postcard to my cousin:
This is what it is like to live in America.
Individual tartlet pans congregate
in the kitchen, chiming my name.
Porcelain fruit boxes float above tables,
sterling silver ice cream cone holders
twirl upside-down on the cat's dozing head.

For years I developed radar against malls.
So what is it that secretly applauds
this army of catalogues marching upon my house?
I could be in the bosom of poverty, still they arrive.
I could be dead, picked apart by vultures,
still they would tell me
what socks to wear in my climbing boots.

Stay true, catalogues, protect me
from the wasteland where whimsy and impulse
never camp.
Be my companion on this journey between dusts,
between vacancy and that smiling stare
that is citizen of every climate
but customer to nothing,
even air.

NORA NARANJO-MORSE

Tradition and Change

My mission was to sell pottery from booth 109,
    so early that morning I drove to San Ildefonso.
I expected this market of arts and crafts to be full,
    a full day in many ways.
    Hundreds of steel-framed booths
    filled the center of the pueblo.
    Cars streamed in at a steady pace,
    while Summer's heat became relentless.
    Oh yes, and there were people, all kinds, from everywhere,
    looking to buy, with spend in their eyes.
    Maybe for pottery.
      I hoped so.
    "Too expensive, Myrtle," I heard a man say to his wife,
    as she reached for one of my clay forms,
    his words pressing her onward to the next booth.
    If it was jewelry they were looking for, this was the place.
    Everything, from finely crafted turquoise inlaid bracelets
    to Mickey Mouse earrings set in mother of pearl,
    his nose in jet, and those shorts of Mickey's
    painted in coral stone.
The Summer's temperature rose as a loudspeaker
    blared continuous news of a disco dance
    being held that evening in another pueblo.
    Warning visitors to stay off the kiva steps,
    and reminding us that Navajo tacos were being sold
    at any one of eight refreshment stands

along the outer wall of the village.
A candidate for governor hurried by,
shaking hands almost desperately
with anyone who looked of voting age.
It was at that moment I turned away, trying to shake off
this state I had entered.
You know, that state of mind that displaces you
for just a second.
Oh yes,
oh yes, this is San Ildefonso Pueblo in the 90's.
All this made me wonder where our people were headed,
what our ancestors would think about a Navajo Taco
going for $3.75.
I thought about changes affecting our tradition,
change and tradition,
on this hot, full day.

MAUREEN OWEN

For Emily (Dickinson)

The girl   working the xerox in the stationery store
has a "thing"   for one of the customers   "I'm in love!"
she blurts to complete strangers buying stamp pad ink.
"Am I shaking!   Last week when he came in   I
stapled my thumb."   It's not just a shift in season
but a hormone that sets the trees off too   from plain
green they go   cheeks flushed   & dropping
everything!
Like the baby bashing through them   hooting   "More!"
&   the radio   announcing   "It's a Sealy Posturepedic
    morning!"
the landscape's gone silly   with abundance of motif   where
the tossed baby   Plunks   into the damp pyramid   &
is gone   from the base a small scuffed shoe
chanting   "Leafs!   Leafs!"   Here
is all the drama of the emperor's flight!   Imperial
dragon robes swept up   porcelains scattered
& the eerie glazed stillness   the soft mist Thudding
where the stately picnic   had been.
Is it a theory of numbers   or just   Quantity
that lifts us   up from under the armpits   with Fred
Astaire singing   in grand finale crescendo   "It
doesn't matter where you get it   as long as you got it!"
                O furious Excesses!
She set her tough skiff   straightaway
into the sea   for love of danger!

tho all the birds have lost   their cover
            & You   O Bald October
                         I knew you   when you
                         still had hair!

JENNIFER M. PIERSON

Thrift Shop Ladies

They carry their long, heavy bosoms inside old sweaters and wear examples of excellent tweed. They are volunteers for Christ or the retarded or some hospital in which their husbands are on the Board. Some give orders, but no one is in charge. Some are not shy, they are too helpful. Their job is routine. Straighten the racks, rehang the shirts, see if anyone needs assistance with the awkward drawer marked "Table Linens."

At St. Albert's in Seattle, men weed through piles of warm suit jackets and beat-down shoes. They are generally ignored by the ladies. With no money to spend, the men drift back out into a cool environ, the dirty streets they call home. I've seen crazy women come in, too. They're nasty, shouting at the dingy yellow wall, or a stained chenille spread. They are toothless, and bulbous. There is a patina of elegance in the ladies and their trade, and the crazy women's yelling seems so unseemly. But they cannot ask them to leave. Not easily.

D.C.'s Junior League Shop ladies love to steal time away to look at a new load of donations. A large box arrives full of gowns from the 1930s. I can hear them sigh at the memory of their own youthful parties. One dress is a sea-green chiffon, embossed with seedpearls. They know they cannot fit into its slender waist. The beadwork on a pale peach number is ogled at, then hung reverently in a private corner.

The ladies in Geneva's Christ Child are good at figures, efficient. They carry calculators to divine the nickels and bills added in taxes. They are precise. The tablets they write upon are as faded and fragile as their slackened cheeks. They do not do a fast trade and their hours are few. Church rooms are for church business, much of the time,

Lunch is a paper sack of sandwich, and coffee from the rectory above. While they eat, they chatter about the downpricing of summer goods. One remarks what good taste I have in dresses. When I exit with my purchases, I hear them argue over the quality of a new piece of costume jewelry. At three o'clock the lights go out and they go their separate ways.

DUANE NIATUM

The Novelty Shop

More grotesque than a row of laundromats,
A haze of pawnshops,
Novel shopkeepers pun Seattle
Like skid row. Outside the entrance
A cigar-store Indian, with the entombed
Stare of a museum sculpture,
Draws the tourists from the East
Into the damp shop of seashore ornaments
For manufactured bores. With the forest
Serenity of a shaman, the black eyes
Of a shaker, Eagle Runner
Abandons the city of red rain, and dives
Into the sea at the end of the pier.

BARON WORMSER

Shoplifting

The store dick lays a hand on your shoulder
Three steps from the exit. He asks what's
In your pockets but it's more like a statement
Than a question. Two candy bars and a roll of film.

Your stomach melts and your heart starts to beat
Like when you used to race on the playground.
He tells you to sit down on the bench by the doors.
Usually there are some old people sitting there

Gabbling about bargains but no one's around
This late in the evening. You expect the manager
To show up and give you a lecture about kids
Nowadays but he doesn't

And when the cop appears he doesn't say
Anything special beyond you'll have to go to court.
When he gives you the paper he's almost smiling
Or he's not there at all, he's not seeing you.

Thoughts, thoughts . . . your head's raw dough
One moment, light as a balloon the next.
They're always playing a song in the background
In these stores that you can't quite identify.

Your foot's tapping to the vacant beat
And after the cop leaves and you
Can leave you don't for some minutes.
You don't even own a camera.

MAURA STANTON

Shoplifters

I'd smoke in the freezer
among the hooked beefsides,
wondering about the shoplifters
who wept when the manager's
nephew tugged them to his office.
He made me search the women.
I found twenty cans of tuna fish
under the skirt of a mother whose son
drowned in a flash flood out west.
Now he haunted her,
begging for mouthfuls of fish.
Candles fell from a nun's sleeves.
She meant to light the route
for tobogganists on the convent hill.
Two old sisters emptied beans
from their big apron pockets,
claiming they cured rheumatism.
Soon I recognized snow
drifting across faces at the door,
watching in the round mirrors
the way hands snatched out
unhesitatingly at onions.
In the mirrors everyone stole,
buttoning coats again, looking
once over their shoulders
while eggs bulged in a mitten

or salt sifted from their hems.
Did they think me an angel
when I glided in my white uniform
down the soap aisle, preventing
some sudden clutch of fingers?
An old man I caught last year
stuffing baloney down his trousers
lived alone in a dim bedroom.
The manager said cupcake papers
blew across his floor—
hundreds, yellow, white & pink.
Now he peers through the window,
watching me bag groceries
for hours until my hands sweat.

LARRY LEVIS

Whitman

*"I say we had better look our nation searchingly in
the face, like a physician diagnosing some deep
disease."*
                                    —Democratic Vistas

"Look for me under your bootsoles."

On Long Island, they moved my clapboard house
Across a turnpike, & then felt so guilty they
Named a shopping center after me!
Teen-agers call me a fool.
Now what I sang stops breathing.

And yet
It was only when everyone stopped believing in me
That I began to live, again—
First in the thin whine of Montana fence wire,
Then in the transparent, cast off garments hung
In the windows of the poorest families,
Then in the glad music of Charlie Parker.
At times now,
I even come back to watch you
From the eyes of a taciturn boy at Malibu.
Across the counter at the beach concession stand,
I sell you hot dogs, Pepsis, cigarettes—
My blond hair long, greasy, & swept back
In a vain old ducktail, deliciously
Out of style.
And no one notices.

Once, I even came back as *me,*
An aging homosexual who ran the Tilt-a-Whirl
At county fairs, the chilled paint on each gondola
Changing color as it picked up speed,
And a Mardi Gras tattoo on my left shoulder.
A few of you must have seen my photographs,
For when you looked back,
I thought you caught the meaning of my stare:
Still water,
Merciless.

A Kosmos. One of the roughs.

Leave me alone.
A father who's outlived his only child.

To find me now will cost you everything.

RICK BURSKY

The Decisions

When our circus finally collapsed the train stopped on thin rails seven miles south of Spiro, Oklahoma. Everyone walked away carrying their possessions in cardboard suitcases. It was morning. Shoes and socks dampened in wet grass between trees. The tattoo lady paused at a river to shave and wash her pastel skin before hitchhiking to a nudist colony in Florida. The Hungarian trapeze artist said he would miss watching earth tumble over his head. So he proposed to the fat lady. He dreamed of moving to Seattle, becoming a window washer, walking on clouds, mops for hands and every night rolling his face over his wife's big white breasts. Harry, the half man half woman, couldn't decide what to do. And since the only thing I knew how to do was put up tents, I joined the army and spent the rest of my life in heavy boots, mistaking the shouts of bullets and trumpets for the clamor of applause trapped below canvas that once was my home.

SUSAN SWARTWOUT

Siamese Twins in Love

A lifetime mirrored: Chang and Eng,
marked into filling the same
space in a freeze-frame of tours
lined with round-eyed faces. You face
the cameras in painful twists,
no smiles. Your eyes,
wild with separate desires
in youth, have opaqued into stoic
reflections. You move as one beast—
even when you marry, buy American
homes only blocks apart, stretch the mirror
until edges bevel into two worlds
you give each other: three-days altered
with each wife, sisters who must
have shared everything.

Nothing can stop us from thinking
of how a wife must straddle
the mirror you make, how one
pair of hips twists to meet her.
And you and you always
smell his same rank sweat
as it laps your skin, his heat
yours, an endless touch
spreading from joined breastbone
to the twinned tightening of nipples,
their points rising like small worms

fattened on lust for hot rain.
Such intimate brotherly love endures
conditional tense. You love to watch
his eyes that mirror yours roll back
as your backs arch, and you undulate
again into beast, want to lay
your tongue down his identical throat.

LOUIS PHILLIPS

My Son Shows Me a Photograph of Michael Jordan Performing a Slam Dunk

What would Jung make of such levitation?
Tho the world is never so sad
As when we are speeding away from it,
Here in the Rialto of Dunk,
One need not invent the awe
In which we hold our heroes. Shrunk

By reality, the need to make a living,
We are mere cobblers
Performing an energy audit,
The measured steps, the hang time,
Here he comes,
Saint of Hoops, *poete maudit*

Creating passionate speech
With his knees,
His arms stretched to the rim
Of astonishments. Bearing noble truths
To the scoreboard & beyond,
The ball appears to be holding him

Above the 2 point crunch. Star chowder
Of instant fame
Spills over him; he is the genius

Of finite air above our heads,
For we shall never in our lives
Do anything this certain, any of us.

WILLIAM HEYEN

Mantle

Mantle ran so hard, they said,
he tore his legs to pieces.
What is this but spirit?

52 homers in '56, the triple crown.
I was a high school junior, batting
fourth behind him in a dream.

I prayed for him to quit, before
his lifetime dropped below .300.
But he didn't, and it did.

He makes Brylcreem commercials now,
models with open mouths draped around him
as they never were in Commerce, Oklahoma,

where the sandy-haired, wide-shouldered boy
stood up against his barn,
lefty for an hour (Ruth, Gehrig),

then righty (DiMaggio),
as his father winged them in,
and the future blew toward him,

now a fastball, now a slow
curve hanging
like a model's smile.

DENIS JOHNSON

The Incognito Lounge

The manager lady of this
apartment dwelling has a face
like a baseball with glasses and pathetically
repeats herself. The man next door
has a dog with a face that talks
of stupidity to the night, the swimming pool
has an empty, empty face.
My neighbor has his underwear on
tonight, standing among the parking spaces
advising his friend never to show
his face around here again.
I go everywhere with my eyes closed and two
eyeballs painted on my face. There is a woman
across the court with no face at all.

———————

They're perfectly visible this evening,
about as unobtrusive as a storm of meteors,
these questions of happiness
plaguing the world.
My neighbor has sent his child to Utah
to be raised by the relatives of friends.
He's out on the generous lawn
again, looking like he's made
out of phosphorus.

———————

The manager lady has just returned
from the nearby graveyard, the last
ceremony for a crushed paramedic.
All day, news helicopters cruised aloft
going whatwhatwhatwhatwhat.
She pours me some boiled
coffee that tastes like noise,
warning me, once and for all,
to pack up my troubles in an old kit bag
and weep until the stones float away.
How will I ever be able to turn
from the window and feel love for her?—
to see her and stop seeing
this neighborhood, the towns of earth,
these tables at which the saints
sit down to the meal of temptations?

———————————

And so on—nap, soup, window,
say a few words into the telephone,
smaller and smaller words.
Some TV or maybe, I don't know, a brisk
rubber with cards nobody knows
how many there are of.
Couple of miserable gerbils
in a tiny white cage, hysterical
friends rodomontading about goals
as if having them liquefied death.
Maybe invite the lady with no face
over here to explain all these elections:
life. Liberty. Pursuit.

———————————

Maybe invite the lady with no face
over here to read my palm,
sit out on the porch here in Arizona

while she touches me.
Last night, some kind
of alarm went off up the street
that nobody responded to.
Small darling, it rang for you.
Everything suffers invisibly,
nothing is possible, in your face.

———————————

The center of the world is closed.
The Beehive, the 8-Ball, the Yo-Yo,
the Granite and the Lightning and the Melody.
Only the Incognito Lounge is open.
My neighbor arrives.
They have the television on.

It's a show about
my neighbor in a loneliness, a light,
walking the hour when every bed is a mouth.
Alleys of dark trash, exhaustion
shaped into residences—and what are the dogs
so sure of that they shout like citizens
driven from their minds in a stadium?
In his fist he holds a note
in his own handwriting,
the same message everyone carries
from place to place in the secret night,
the one that nobody asks you for
when you finally arrive, and the faces
turn to you playing the national anthem
and go blank, that's
what the show is about, that message.

———————————

I was raised up from tiny
childhood in those purple hills,

right slam on the brink of language,
and I claim it's just as if
you can't do anything to this moment,
that's how inextinguishable
it all is. Sunset,
Arizona, everybody waiting
to get arrested, all very
much an honor, I assure you.
Maybe invite the lady with no face
to plead my cause, to get
me off the hook or name
me one good reason.
The air is full of megawatts

and the megawatts are full of silence.
She reaches to the radio like St. Theresa.

———————————

Here at the center of the world
each wonderful store cherishes
in its mind undeflowerable
mannequins in a pale, electric light.
The parking lot is full,
everyone having the same dream
of shopping and shopping
through an afternoon
that changes like a face.

But these shoppers of America—
carrying their hearts toward the bluffs
of the counters like thoughtless purchases,
walking home under the sea,
standing in a dark house at midnight
before the open refrigerator, completely
transformed in the light . . .

———————————

Every bus ride is like this one,
in the back the same two uniformed boy scouts
de-pantsing a little girl, up front
the woman whose mission is to tell the driver
over and over to shut up.
Maybe you permit yourself to find
it beautiful on this bus as it wafts
like a dirigible toward suburbia
over a continent of saloons,
over the robot desert that now turns
purple and comes slowly through the dust.
This is the moment you'll seek
the words for over the imitation
and actual wood of successive
tabletops indefatigably,
when you watched a baby child
catch a bee against the tinted glass
and were married to a deep
comprehension and terror.

PAUL ZIMMER

Romance

This frightened, horny boy
Sits in a jazz club full of
Jungle ferns and leopard skins.

A piano trio is playing,
Dulcet and precise,
"My One and Only Love."

Hank Jones or Billy Taylor?
Al Haig? Ellis Larkins?
It does not matter.

What counts is this song
About something we do not even
Presume to hope for anymore.

Just in time, this wistful,
Tipsy boy hears about love
So sure it lasts a lifetime.

M A R K   D O T Y

Days of 1981

Cambridge Street, summer,
and a boy in a blue bandanna brought the bartender
flowers: delphiniums, splendid, blackened

in the dim room, though it was still afternoon, "tea
dance," in the heat of early July. Men in too-tight jeans
—none of them dancing—watched

the black women singing. Secret advocates of our hearts,
they urged us on as they broke apart
in painterly chaos on the video screen,

gowns and wigs, perfectly timed gestures
becoming bits of iridescent weather
in the club's smoked atmosphere. The Supremes

—by then historical, lushly ascetic—then the endless
stream of women we loved, emblematic, reckless
in their attachments, or so the songs would have us think.

The man I met, slight and dark as Proust, a sultry flirt,
introduced himself because he liked my yellow shirt.
I don't remember who bought who drinks,

or why I liked him; I think it was simply
that I *could*. The heady rush of quickly
leaving together, late sun glaring over the Charles,

those last white sails blinding: it was so easy,
and strangely exhilarating, and free
as the women singing: a tidal, glimmering whirl

into which you could ease down, without thinking,
and simply be swept away. I was ready and waiting
to be swept. After the subway ride,

he knelt in front of me on the bleachers
in an empty suburban park, and I reached
for anything to hold onto, my head thrown back

to blueblack sky rinsed at the rim
with blazing city lights, then down to him:
relentless, dazzling, anyone. The smokestacks

and office towers loomed, a half-lit backdrop
beyond the baseball diamond. I didn't want him to ever stop,
and he left me breathless and unsatisfied.

He was a sculptor, and for weeks afterward I told myself
I loved him, because I'd met a man and wasn't sure
I could meet another—I'd never tried—

and because the next morning, starting
off to work, the last I saw of him, he gave me a heart,
ceramic, the marvel of a museum school show

his class had mounted. No one could guess
how he'd fired hollow clay entirely seamless
and kept it from exploding. I thought it beautiful, though

I was wrong about so much: him,
my prospects, the charm of the gift.
Out of context, it was a cool,

lumpish thing, earth-toned, lop-sided,
incapable of standing on its own. I propped
it up with books, then left it somewhere, eventually,

though I don't mind thinking of it now,
when I don't have the first idea where it's gone.
I called him more than twice.

If I knew where he was, even his last name,
(something French?) I might call again
to apologize for my naive

persistence, my lack of etiquette,
my ignorance of the austere code of tricks.
I didn't know then how to make love like that.

I thought of course we'd go on learning
the fit of chest to chest, curve to curve.
I didn't understand the ethos, the drama

of the search,
the studied approach to touch
as brief and recklessly enjambed

as the magic songs: *Give me just a little more time,*
I'm so excited, I will survive.
Nothing was promised, nothing sustained

or lethal offered. I wish I'd kept the heart.
Even the emblems of our own embarrassment
become acceptable to us, after a while,

evidence of someone we'd once have wished to erase:
a pottery heart,
an unrecaptured thing that might represent

the chancy exhilaration of a day, years ago
—1981—bleached sails on the Charles blowing,
the blueblack women in their rapture on the screen,

their perfected longing and release.
The astonishing flowers, seething
a blue I could barely see.

DAVID BAKER

8-Ball at the Twilite

for Ed Byrne

The team of Budweiser horses
circling the clock above the bar
must have run a thousand miles already tonight.
What a great place they must want to go,
to work so hard in the smoky air. They've kept on running
though our game fell apart, though the music turned
bad, even though the cowboys at the corner booth
slugged it out over a halter-
topped waitress and had to leave.

It's late now and we should go too.
But we've got one more quarter on the table-edge,
pressing our luck, and half a pitcher
still cool enough to drink.
Connie Francis may say she loves us, if we stay.
So we pass the nub of chalk between us again,
rubbing the last of it over our tips
as a new rack of balls explodes,
running hard for the far green corners.

JIM DANIELS

Ted's Bar and Grill

for Russell Rock

Every night at this place
with one pool table, one pinball machine
we shuffle our greasy boots
up to the bar where Jeannie serves up drinks
with her long blond hair and nice ass.
She's engaged to "a good guy—
he don't hang out in bars"
and she don't have no trouble handling the drunks
because she's so sweet even the drunkest pigs
get shamed by her blushes.

And there's this retarded guy Herbert
with a screwed up face
who can't talk right and drools a lot.
He's always trying to pick up Fat Mary
who needs two bar stools, one for each check.
She's always telling him
that she'll bring her boyfriend in
and every time she does
he puts on his sad dog face and starts to moan.
Nobody call stand the noise
so we end up dragging him out the door.
We all know Mary ain't got no boyfriend
and she's lonely as hell

and we're all waiting for the night
she'll get drunk enough so Herbert don't seem retarded
and take him home with her.

Then there's Marty
who just about owns the pool table—
nobody can beat him and no one will play him
but he won't go nowhere else to play.
And old Ted the owner
he just raised prices again and we're pissed
but it's hard to bitch at Jeannie
and Ted hardly comes around anymore
except to kick us out and close up.

Not much excitement here—
not since Jerry kicked the shit out of his boy
when he came in all high on dope
to try and borrow his old man's car.
That was some fight—but a drinker always beats a doper,
everybody knows that.

When the bar closes, I drift on home
and go to bed. Some days I feel
real stupid about myself and my drinking
and can't fall asleep.
I think about going in to work
with a head on again.

I got to stop hanging out at Ted's.
Some nights I try to stay home after work
but then I start thinking
that maybe I'll miss something—
that maybe somebody will beat Marty
or pick up Jeannie or kick Ted's ass
or maybe Herbert will really pick up Mary
walk out the door holding her hand
looking back at me with his goofy face

finally smiling
and twisting my own sour mouth
into a grin.

WILLIAM MATTHEWS

A Story Often Told in Bars:
The *Reader's Digest* Version

First I was born and it was tough on Mom.
Dad felt left out. There's much I can't recall.
I seethed my way to speech and said a lot
of things: some were deemed cute. I was so small
my likely chance was growth, and so I grew.
Long days in school I filled, like a spring creek,
with boredom. Sex I discovered soon
enough, I now think. Sweet misery!

There's not enough room in a poem so curt
to get me out of adolescence, yet
I'm nearing fifty with a limp, and dread
the way the dead get stacked up like a cord
of wood. Not much of a story, is it?
The life that matter's not the one I've led.

ANITA ENDREZZE PROBST

The Stripper

I

On the stage, mirrored many times,
my body is cubed and squared,
sequined and feathered, bare
and rounded, bright and hot
under the lights and sweaty stares;
drum roll, grinding hips, pivot
swing, cupping my warm hands slowly
up to my breast, slipping off
the red laced bra in twenty wet sighs
unfastening silk underwear to reveal
skin dark fur, musty stroke of things,
while they grasp their brown bottles
and I groan, opening my mouth,
looking not at the men below
but at the luminous green exit sign.

II

During the intermissions, I walk over
the thrown coins on the floor, mostly dimes,
into the bathroom to replace
my breasts, flick ashes into toilet bowls
put back my underwear Newberry pink
and fluff out the black feathers:
I always lose some every time.

These lights show the bones carving
through the finish of my face:
Jukebox songs knife years across my lips,
echoing in the hollows of my cheeks,
rattling my tongue dry,
but the only music in here
is the gargle of the toilets
and the sound of its blue beat
matching the wine in my veins.

THOMAS RABBITT

The Dancing Sunshine Lounge

The calendar is ironic. The stripper dances
On my table, her toes awash in beer.
Ash Wednesday drags in once a year. This year
Thursday brings a dust storm from the west.
The day is airborne Oklahoma, a breast
That Lent would like to bare against the east.
The sun comes closer. A silver cast—
Her shield, this target—tarnishes the air.
The stripper's memorial body chances
My hands, my broken glass. She can't care.
We are washing down traildust, we rich dead
Who have blown in, frantic, on the wind,
And she thinks we must be paralyzed with fear.
She can't care. She loves us each like a friend.

ROBIN BECKER

Dreaming at the Rexall Drug

In Wyoming, at the confluence
of Clear and Piney creeks, I find myself
watching low clouds mass above the Bighorns.
If I were to get on the bicycle
and ride to Buffalo,

I'd saunter into the Rexall Drug
and order a root beer float, I'd fill out
a contest form to win a thoroughbred,
as I did every week in my eighth year,
in love with the bay in the plate glass window.

In Buffalo, Wyoming, an America
my Russian grandmother never imagined,
we are standing before the cosmetics
counter, and she is testing Revlon
lipsticks to find the perfect shade of peach.

I drift toward the comic books where Lois Lane
is repeatedly rescued and flies—
past skyscrapers and suspension bridges—
as I do in my dreams.
My grandmother takes my hand and we walk.

At the house it's 1955 and
my father has the thick black hair he lost
before I was born. He leads us to the

patio where Chinese lanterns sway
like soft paper crowns. All the neighbors

I will grow to love are laughing and floating
in the buoyant atmosphere, and here comes
my mother in a party dress, holding
my baby sister. I've not learned to read
their faces for bankruptcy or grief.

As far as I know, everyone will live
forever, and little girls like me
will continue to win racehorses
from Rexall, where my grandmother will stand,
twisting lipstick tubes, discovering one

imperfect color after another.

JASON SHINDER

Waitress

There is a table in the back where she opens
her mouth to red lipstick, lets her eyes down
for a touch of blue mascara, and rests

her bunioned feet. Six more hours
before she can sip Coca-Cola and sleep
in front of her father's new Magnavox 14 inch Black & White,

Milton Berle running across the screen.
She touched Mr. Berle's hand once in 1948
when he raised his right arm for her

and a roast beef sandwich. The world shrieked,
rang in promise. She knows it was then the twitching began
in her left eye. Esther is still

waiting tables at Dubrows. Sadie still hanging coats
at Sutters. Sunday, she's got her cousin Lenny's
green Chevrolet. The tall kitchen doors swing back

and forth, parting the hair on her forehead.
She can taste the salt at the back of her throat
thinking of the man

who will lean into her one night. Not the girl
smiling, balancing three bowls of soup on her left arm,
but a woman who would claim all beauty hers,

not to keep it, but to hold it long enough to change.

RODNEY JONES

On the Bearing of Waitresses

Always I thought they suffered, the way they huffed
through the Benzedrine light of waffle houses,
hustling trays of omelettes, gossiping by the grill,
or pruning passes like the too prodigal buds of roses,
and I imagined each come home to a trailer court,
the yard of bricked-in violets, the younger sister
pregnant and petulant at her manicure, the mother
with her white Bible, the father sullen in his corner.
Wasn't that the code they telegraphed in smirks?
And wasn't this disgrace, to be public and obliged,
observed like germs or despots about to be debunked?
Unlikely brides, apostles in the gospel of stereotypes,
their future was out there beyond the parked trucks,
between the beer joints and the sexless church,
the images we'd learned from hayseed troubadours—
perfume, grease, and the rending of polarizing loves.
But here in the men's place, they preserved a faint
decorum of women and, when they had shuffled past us,
settled in that realm where the brain approximates
names and rounds off the figures under uniforms.
Not to be honored or despised, but to walk as spies would,
with almost alien poise in the imperium of our disregard,
to go on steadily, even on the night of the miscarriage,
to glide, quick smile, at the periphery of appetite.
And always I had seen them listening, as time brought
and sent them, hovering and pivoting as the late

orders turned strange, *blue garden, brown wave.* Spit
in the salad, wet socks wrung into soup, and this happened.
One Sunday morning in a truckstop in Bristol, Virginia,
a rouged and pancaked half-Filipino waitress
with hair dyed the color of puffed wheat and mulberries
singled me out of the crowd of would-be bikers
and drunken husbands guzzling coffee to sober up
in time to cart their disgusted wives and children
down the long street to the First Methodist Church.
Because I had a face she trusted, she had me wait
that last tatter of unlawful night that hung there
and hung there like some cast-off underthing
caught on the spikes of a cemetery's wrought-iron fence.
And what I had waited for was no charm of flesh,
not the hard seasoning of luck, or work, or desire,
but all morning, in the sericea by the filthy city lake,
I suffered her frightened lie, how she was wanted
in Washington by the CIA, in Vegas by the FBI—
while time shook us like locks that would not break.
And I did not speak, though she kept pausing to look
back across one shoulder, as though she were needed
in the trees, but waxing her slow paragraphs into
chapters, filling the air with her glamour and her shame.

MARKHAM JOHNSON

The All-Night Diner

Tonight, you will not tire
of waitresses with free refills.
The eggs you ordered a decade ago
may never appear. It doesn't matter.
In the next booth, James Dean
punches the jukebox on the wall,
and whispers in your ear, "no one returns
from the all-night diner,"
and you believe him.
The selection is endless,
and eternity begins with "Teen Angel,"
then "Dead Man's Curve." In back,
a medley of sunburned tourists,
just off the boat to paradise,
select Don Ho melodies
and piña coladas, or coffee
with miniature cows for cream.
Patience is not a virtue here,
but a way of watching
the waitresses in their slow
unhurried gait. They have been here
since the beginning and know
just how to walk without
bumping the stools,
or even lying down to sleep
on marbled counters, or wondering

when the pale moon will finally
rise off the front glass
to take its place in the neon firmament,
as someone pulls the shades
and turns over the vacancy sign to full.

SHARON BRYAN

Lunch with Girl Scouts

. . . the spirit intercedes . . . most eloquently on our behalf . . .

These ten-year-olds all want other names
than their own. I'm Heather, but call me
Laura, says the one who should have played
Lolita in the movie. Her lips are damp
and unbitten. My mother still has a bracelet
she made in camp, with her fantasy name,
Louise, in orange beads. Names can break
our hearts. I've been invited to lunch
with Girl Scouts, to talk to them about
poetry. They're braver than I am, to have gotten
this far. Longing for a uniform,
I spent three weeks as a Brownie. The leader
talked about fly-ups. Soon we would all
fly-up. This meant a plane ride,
or becoming an angel. Either way,
we might die. I quit, with nothing
to show for my torment but a cryptic
pin. The others flew-up—they were
promoted. Once more I'd misfigured
the language I loved. *Round John virgin*,
we sang at Christmas. And I believed
that if I rode my thick Schwinn down
the right alley in springtime, I'd be,
as the song promised, *out at the old
ball game*. There, in the stands, gulping

popcorn, cheering for the Bees. Today
I followed a map into the suburbs,
suddenly shy as I was as a child
but old as the teachers we considered
foreign countries. I begin to take hold
of their various names, but by lunchtime
I haven't said anything useful. My hostess
and I eat quiche, the girls spaghetti.
Pasghetti. They giggle. One says
a two-line poem, and another answers
with four. They're quoting a recent book
they've all read. Each recites
her favorite while the others bounce
on their hands. None of this
is for me. Somehow they've found
a long one they all know and are almost
shouting it in unison. They pull up
their socks without missing a beat,
spill out of the room like marbles.
I stare into my coffee. When was I last
so full of love? So innocent of error?

MICHAEL PETTIT

Vanna White's Bread Pudding

If not famous ourselves, oh let us
nudge up against stars and starlets

everybody knows, everybody envies
for all the sweet attention they receive.

Like when in Mother's Restaurant
a table opened up for us, lucky guys,

next to the table in the corner
where three good-looking women sat,

attended by some sharp fellow
and looks from all the other patrons.

Damn if we didn't set down our gumbo
and red beans and cold Dixie beer

beside the TV personalities in town
to do business and enjoy good food.

Damn if it wasn't Vanna White herself
sitting there, in the flesh, in pink,

face from the Wheel of Fortune weeknights,
figure that turned the letters round

and turned all the heads in Mother's
and drew a chorus of whispers—

Vanna White, Vanna White, Vanna White
next to us, not an arm's length away.

And when the owner himself came over
insisting she try the famous bread pudding—

despite her protests, despite her trim waist,
despite the waste she hated to see—

damn if Vanna didn't turn, smiling,
and offer her bread pudding to me. To me!

Damn if I didn't say thanks, and take it.
Damn if it wasn't sweet, buttery, hot,

and therefore gone in a wink, like a star falling
into my heretofore but no more anonymous lap.

THOM TAMMARO

'mericn fst fd

sld bar 1.99 + drnk

dbl ches lrg fri pep   hlf chic slaw drnk   burg fri coke

fish sand slaw + drnk   ches bac burg   pork fri frit

burg fri pop   pan fri fritr pot sald drnk

specl: yr choice: .69   tuna   sal sand
chic   sal sand
egg   sal sand
ham   sal sand
turkey   sal sand

hlf brost chic slaw mash pot sml drnk   lrg shake brgr fri   cig1.69 pk

tatr tots   sal bar w/pop   hot chic wings 1.99

cigarettesbeerpopgasmeatgroceryicebaitslusheeslurpeemilkbreadhotsandsicecreamhotdogs

all u care 2 eat

JIM DANIELS

Short-Order Cook

An average joe comes in
and orders thirty cheeseburgers and thirty fries.

I wait for him to pay before I start cooking.
He pays.
He ain't no average joe.

The grill is just big enough for ten rows of three.
I slap the burgers down
throw two buckets of fries in the deep frier
and they pop pop spit spit . . .
psss . . .
The counter girls laugh.
I concentrate.
It is the crucial point—
they are ready for the cheese:
my fingers shake as I tear off slices
toss them on the burgers/fries done/dump/
refill buckets/burgers ready/flip into buns/
beat that melting cheese/wrap burgers in plastic/
into paper bags/fries done/dump/fill thirty bags/
bring them to the counter/wipe sweat on sleeve
and smile at the counter girls.
I puff my chest out and bellow:
"Thirty cheeseburgers, thirty fries!"
They look at me funny.

I grab a handful of ice, toss it in my mouth
do a little dance and walk back to the grill.
Pressure, responsibility, success,
thirty cheeseburgers, thirty fries.

JANET SYLVESTER

Arrowhead Christian Center
and No-Smoking Luncheonette

Each Saturday, our father downtown to work,
Eloise tagged along to watch me look
through flaked-gold letters at Arthur Benson, the Baptist.
While I dressed in a magenta sweater
and navy-blue felt skirt with a white poodle
pasted on it, she would roll her eyes,
stick out her tongue and make gagging noises at my choice
of clothes. This Saturday, Arthur wore chino pants
and white bucks and a pullover with no shirt underneath.
First, I lit one of my mother's Old Golds.
Arthur never looked up from his pamphlet.
Then I leaned on the revolving door,
hoping Eloise would go home, where I sent her.

The luncheonette smelled of cooking coffee.
"Arthur," I said, positioning my chest against the counter,
"give me whatever I sign to prove I testify with you
to Jesus." Arthur sauntered over to me
with a sheet of yellow paper that said:
I, blank blank, room for my name, *do renounce fornication,
smoking, dancing, and so on. I will take on the Lord.*
I signed. He asked me out. I had heard that about Arthur.
"Oh Arthur, you're so crazy," I said
as we warmed up his white Chevrolet.
Later, when all the windows were steamy, he kissed me
without opening his lips, and showed my hand

how far it could go inside his pants.
Arthur stretched his arms across the seat back
as I bent, hair falling around my mouth and what it did,
my head wedged against the steering wheel.
"Blackhaired bitch," he whispered, "your hair's like wire."
I had never chugged anything till then
but knew how much, sometimes, you have to swallow in life
to prove a point.

Halfway down the street,
I could see my father waiting on the porch.
Eloise had spied on me and then went home
to tell about that paper.
When he finished hitting me,
Daddy pulled me out into the yard under his fruit trees.
It was only February, but already
there were crocuses uncurling in the flowerbeds.
When he put his arm around me,
all I could think about was Arthur,
how he bucked and crushed my head over and over again
onto his body.
Daddy wasn't saying much so I identified a constellation
that sinks down in the spring, Orion,
and wondered how much loafers stretch from standing
in muddy grass, and saw the moon go in and out
my father's breath. I wedged my head then
into that little cradle below his shoulder, pretending
I would never go near the luncheonette again.

BARON WORMSER

By-Products

The legion hall in Atherton contains
Three unclean couches, more than fifty uncomfortable chairs,
   Seven brands of less-than-good whiskey,
A tomcat with one glaucous eye named "Ike,"
Stagnant windowless air, and more often than not

   My legless friend, Stan, who, unlike most
Of the human race in this county and beyond, is content to go
   Unsaved. He drinks ginger-ale, talks about sex
In a voice of awe and disgust, and plays cribbage
For a buck a game. "Here sits," he says sometimes

   Out of the blue and to no one special, "one of
The by-products of Vietnamization" but no one hushes up the way
   They used to because everyone there's a veteran
Of one sort or another, and who, in fact, knows shit
About Korea anymore or, for that matter, Tarawa

   As witnessed by Charley Levesque who, though
Here, never came home? Friday nights it's cards and some
   Mediocre eight-ball and later talk which doesn't
Always wind up back in 'Nam but more often hovers
Between there and here, say in some Pentagon general's

   So-called mind or a television show or a girl's
Smile at a football game fifteen years ago. Neither of us ever had
   Much talent for optimism nor, for that matter,

Rage. Our insignificance lulls us, and we know it
Could all happen again, whatever it was, an obligation

    Split by a moment; or as with me, a lifetime of
Moments, each one praying nothing will happen. Living is the job no
    One's particularly good at, and somedays Stan says
He feels more here than anyone, because he gave something
Up, because there's a difference between being hurt and being afraid.

WILLIAM HATHAWAY

Why That's Bob Hope

The comedian, holding a chunk of flaming shale.
If only *Der Bingle* could see him now! He looked
so puffed and sleepy in that Texaco hardhat,
I could've popped a fuse. Well, like the oil,

here today and gone today. In *my* good old days
Hope was on Sullivan's "shew" so often us kids
dropped TV for longhair sex and smoking weeds.
What a mistake! But now we're past our wild phase

and Bob's back with this burning rock, funny
for a change. No, no old quips now about Dean's double
vision, Phyllis Diller's breasts or Sinatra's aging treble.
He says if we all squeeze the rock together real money

will drip out. We'll live real good and still afford a war
where he'll bust our boys' guts on tour in El Salvador.

CHARLES BERNSTEIN

Of Time and the Line

George Burns likes to insist that he always
takes the straight lines; the cigar in his mouth
is a way of leaving space between the
lines for a laugh. He weaves lines together
by means of a picaresque narrative;
not so Hennie Youngman, whose lines are strict-
ly paratactic. My father pushed a
line of ladies' dresses—not down the street
in a pushcart but upstairs in a fact'ry
office. My mother has been more concerned
with her hemline. Chairman Mao put forward
Maoist lines, but that's been abandoned (most-
ly) for the East-West line of malarkey
so popular in these parts. The prestige
of the iambic line has recently
suffered decline, since it's no longer so
clear who "I" am, much less who *you* are. When
making a line, better be double sure
what you're lining in & what you're lining
out & which side of the line you're on; the
world is made up so (Adam didn't so much
name as delineate). Every poem's got
a prosodic lining, some of which will
unzip for summer wear. The lines of an
imaginary are inscribed on the
social flesh by the knifepoint of history.

Nowadays, you can often spot a work
of poetry by whether it's in lines
or no; if it's in prose, there's a good chance
it's a poem. While there is no lesson in
the line more useful than that of the pick-
et line, the line that has caused the most ad-
versity is the bloodline. In Russia
everyone is worried about long lines;
back in the USA, it's strictly soup-
lines. "Take a chisel to write," but for an
actor a line's got to be cued. Or, as
they say in math, it takes two lines to make
an angle but only one lime to make
a Margarita.

ALBERT GOLDBARTH

The Counterfeit Earth!

1. Ballpoint C & C

It's 2157. Two adventuring spacemen rocketing home
are stupefied by a vision of side-by-side twin Earths
—one (which one?) being a "mega-televised mock-up"
concocted by wily Terran scientists as proof against
a rapidly approaching alien warfleet: if their test ship comes
within 1,000 miles of the duplicate planet, hidden
"atomic batteries" will fry it with a bolt and,
chain-reactioning, will fry the entire enemy armada.
Fine. But what about our heroes, caught in space
and facing the same impossible choice, huh? Well,

*

it's 1963. I close that comic book. I'm 15: there
are realer pressures. I'm in a men's-room stall and scrawling
ballpoint cocks and cunts (these loopy doodles are miles
away from being "penises" or "vaginas") on the already
much-cocked sheetrock. Is it criminal
defacing? is it primal confrontation with The Great
and Sacred Mysteries? etc.—I'll get to that. For
now, it's one more 15-year-old man/boy overbrimmed
with the whelm of daily life, and venting it, quickly, in language
as old as the first flame-licked cave walls. It's

79 A.D. This same symmetrical, cilia-rayed, puffed pout
and roughly bulbous protrusion are being scratched
on the wine-house walls of Pompeii. Amid the archwayed
garden-walks of the gentry, these appear. Around
the laurel-bordered frescoes of the gods, and on the altar bases,
these are drawn, and plastered over, and redrawn.
Outside the Temple of Isis, and there in a farther corner
of the Villa of Papyrus Scrolls, while hair is coiffed,
and wax tablets are smoothed, and the suckling pig is spitted . . .
A skull. Wings. Labia. Ass cheeks. Lightning. Erections.

2. Survey of Types

Now that graffiti *is* art, and wins its fellowships
and coffee-table books and tv interviews like any art, we
might want to remember its first appearance *in* art, in
Giacomo Balla's 1902 oil on canvas, *Bankruptcy*,
a close-up of two massive wooden panels of a doorway
so long unused, they've become a museum of chalk
streetscribbling: gutterscribbling really, it's so
crudely splenetic, so schematized an explosion
of bawdy comedy, despair, and rage, so willing to place its
dignity in chalk used like a tripe-plucking knife

*

—not a "counterfeit," no, but a *counterweight*, Earth
that balances the galleries of oil portraits of merchant princes
and dandily pampered nudes, and came before. Now where
to draw the line between such raw, guerrilla lines and
the equally raw and yet grandly pictoreligious scratchwork
unto The Mother Goddess or The Priapic Shaman, in Ice Age
stick-and-circle art we've trained our later eyes to see
as devotional? We never know; the lines behind the fierce, illicit

scribbles of the Balla painting, Dickens understood: the deprived,
the sellers of their own children, the feral, the hunted-down

*

—yet turn the nearest corner, and these on-the-lam inscriptions
are a randy celebration, flanked by a joyful crayoned fireworks
and an inky goatee on the chin of a famous cabaret chanteuse.
Perhaps all we can say of them is what *they* say, always,
under what they say: "I'm here, my peck of elements is charged
      and cohering,
I make things." In Greece, at Sunium, at the temple of Poseidon,
Dr. Edward Dodwell slept in a cavern, sketching the view,
examining the columns both toppled and standing. Rose Macauley
writes: "Did Dodwell carve his name? Nine years later,
Byron, of course, did so." Whistling. Nonchalant. Of course.

3. From Somewhere Beyond the Moon

And Dickens visited Pompeii, saw the stone jots
of its stopped-watch life, "the chafing of the bucket-rope
in the stone rim of the well, the marks of drinking-vessels
on the stone counter of the wineshop . . ." A soldier's just
paid for his red that, somewhere between the amphora
and his cup, gets watered. But what the hell. The mountain's a little
angry today, but what the hell with that too. This
afternoon he's lush with feeling as much as with drink,
and on his way home lifts his marking-stone and,
at a back but very public wall, unlooses:

*

this same set of cartoon genitalia our 15-year-old does,
while the earliest States-release of the Beatles *yeah-yeah-yeahs*
through the bar-&-grill air. I remember that boy so well,
his openness to moil and flux . . . Bob Dylan nasally singing
"The Times They Are A-Changin'" can bring him to his knees
(when he's alone in his room) with emotion from somewhere

beyond the moon. Or so can something he and his friends have learned
to call "injustice." And as for the milky, silky cling
to Laura Maggowicz's ass-cleft as she passes in the hall . . . !
It's all too much. By now he's home for the night, and reopens:

*

this, his nickel-bin (thus coverless) copy of
Mystery in Space (for January 1957) which he completes
before sleep pulls him into its own enormous darkness and stars.
Our goodguy rocketeers, it turns out, touch down surely
on the real Earth, but simulate exploding, with jolts of energy
channeled off their engine. Wholly flimflammed, the waiting aliens
zero-in on the *other* planet, and consequently get flashed
into atomic cinders: happy ending, goodnight. Oh, and how
did our heroes know?—well, only the real Earth showed "the Great
Wall of China, which can be seen from space." So

Zen: the writing *is* the wall.

PAUL VIOLI

Harold and Imogene

The beautiful Imogene is finally alone
with him. She wants to tell him she knows
he is a Martian but that she also loves
him and his secret is safe with her.
As he turns and hands her her drink she blurts
out her confession, throwing her arms
around his neck. His response petrifies her.
He becomes totally rigid. A horrible
realisation stuns her to sobriety. She mumbles
the words before they are formed in her mind:
"You come from another galaxy, don't you?
You're probably different from us, aren't you?
You've been transformed to look like us, haven't you?
Why for all I know, I'm repulsive to you!"
She faints. Harold knows she will tell the other
house guests that he is secretly a Martian
and endanger the success of his mission.
He knows what he must do. He unclasps
the cuff-link that contains a vial of de-metabolizing
fluid. He drops it. It shatters on the floor.
Panicked, he gets down and starts licking the fluid
off the tile. It is a futile exercise.
Something else stops him, however. He has noticed
his reflection on the shiny surface. Imogene,
that very afternoon, had waxed those tiles
with SUPER BRITE, the all new floor wax

that is the nation's leading seller.
Harold stares at his gleaming visage.
He realizes he will be wearing that mask
for the rest of his mortal days on planet Earth.
His dejection is profound. He stands up, knocks
his head against the mantelpiece and sobs.

JAMES TATE

The Motorcyclists

My cuticles are a mess. Oh honey, by the way,
did you like my new negligee? It's a replica
of one Kim Novak wore in some movie or other.
I wish I had a footlong chili dog right now.
Do you like fireworks, I mean not just on the 4th
of July, but fireworks anytime? There are people
like that, you know. They're like people who like
orchestra music, listen to it anytime of day.
Lopsided people, that's what my father calls them.
Me, I'm easy to please. I like pingpong and bobcats,
shatterproof drinking glasses, the smell of kerosene,
the crunch of carrots. I like caterpillars and
whirlpools, too. What I hate most is being the first
one at the scene of a bad accident.

Do I smell like garlic? Are we still in Kansas?
I once had a chiropractor make a pass at me,
did I ever tell you that? He said that your spine
is happiest when you're snuggling. Sounds kind
of sweet now when I tell you, but he was a creep.
Do you know that I have never understood what they meant
by grassy knoll. It sounds so idyllic, a place to go
to dream your life away, not kill somebody. They
should have called it something like the "grudging notch."
But I guess that's life. What is it they always say?
"It's always the sweetest ones that break your heart."
You getting hungry yet, hon? I am. When I was seven

I sat in our field and ate an entire eggplant
right off the vine. Dad loves to tell that story,

but I still can't eat eggplant. He says I'll be the first
woman President, it'd be a waste since I talk so much.
Which do you think the fixtures are in the bathroom
at the White House, gold or brass? It'd be okay with me
if they were just brass. Honey, can we stop soon?
I really hate to say it but I need a lady's room.

CATRON GRIEVES

Indian Car

Driving to the Winnebago pow-wow, across Iowa in the August evening
we have left Iowa City in an "Indian Car." You probably know the type,
good transmission, bald tires, cracked windshield, Janet Jackson on the
      radio,
the kids' dance clothes, handbeaded vests and moccasins safe in the
      trunk.

I have been very homesick, so Janelle said, "you better come stay
with my family, and go to the pow-wow."
So, we are in the car talking about becoming more like the people
at home, the closer we get—we take off our educated voices,
we talk about alcoholic fathers, too many people who need the too
      few jobs
on the reservation, babies born to highschool mothers, and we talk
about losing the native languages. "How do you say that." We have
      asked
our mothers, and too many times they say, "Oh,
I used to know that, but I can't remember anymore."

She tells me her name is Wau Sau Nu Qua,
Sunlight Shining Through The Storm Clouds.
She tells me her grandmother named her on the fourth day.
Halfway between Des Moines and Omaha at 10:45 P.M. we stop
at an all night truckstop.—You know the drill—gas, pee,
stuff for the kids to eat. We don't leave the kids asleep
alone in the car so we take turns

going in, the attendant is a woman, older, one trucker talking to his
    wife
on the telephone, and five local types drive up in an old car. Look like
trouble about to happen, pretty soon.

We are two women aware that because we are "Indian women"
with babies in the car, trouble could come.
When they stood too close, we left without food.
With the truckstop, "WE STAY OPEN ALL NIGHT" in the rearview
    mirror,
we talk again, this time it's "why is it that you can go to college,
and no matter how many VISA cards you carry, sometimes you don't
    feel
free to use them in the middle of America."

We pay the toll across the bridge into Nebraska,
a deer crosses our headlights, before we pull into the driveway,
the porchlight comes on.
We are home and it is after one A.M. We stay up to talk.
We play a video. Little sister has just graduated from Marine
training in South Carolina. In her uniform she is a warrior,
in the tradition of warriors.
In the hot Carolina sun she is proud, we see her resolve,
she will keep the country safe. Her mother talks
about her highschool days. How all the girls went to college.
And we sleep.

At breakfast, the men at the table are speaking of Viet Nam, and Ko-
    rea,
about honor and dishonor, and the old traditions, corn soup, and the
    dances
and giveaways, to honor the war dead.

In the afternoon we women go to the mall in Sioux City,
for a perm, and to shop at Sears. Eat Chinese food.
Representatives of all the branches of the military
are at the dance. I like the jingle dances almost as much

as the squaw dance. And Sunday night we are on our way back
to Iowa City, from Native land. I worry
that we will not find a safe stop
to gas up this "Indian Car."

DAVID BOTTOMS

In the Black Camaro

Through the orange glow of taillights, I crossed
the dirt road, entered the half-mile
of darkness and owl screech, tangled briar
and fallen trunk,
followed the yellow beam of Billy Parker's flashlight
down the slick needle-hill,
half crawling, half sliding and kicking
for footholds, tearing up
whole handfuls of scrub brush and leaf-mulch
until I jumped the mud bank, walked the ankle-deep creek,
the last patch of pine, the gully,
and knelt at the highway
stretching in front of Billy Parker's house,
spotted the black Chevy Camaro parked under a maple
not fifty feet from the window
where Billy Parker rocked in and out of view,
studied in the bad light of a table lamp
the fine print of his Allstate policy.

I cut the flashlight, checked up and down the highway.
Behind me the screech growing distant, fading
into woods, but coming on
a network of tree frogs signaling along the creek.
Only that, and the quiet of my heels
coming down on asphalt
as I crossed the two-lane and stood at the weedy edge
of Billy Parker's yard, stood
in the lamp glare of the living room

where plans were being made to make me rich
and thought of a boat and Johnson outboard,
of all the lures on a K-Mart wall, of reels
and graphite rods, coolers of beer, weedy banks
of dark fishy rivers,
and of Billy Parker rocking in his chair,
studying his coverage, his bank account,
his layoff at Lockheed, his wife laboring
in the maternity ward of the Cobb General Hospital.

For all of this, I crouched in the shadow of fender
and maple, popped the door on the Camaro,
and found in the faint house-light drifting
through the passenger's window
the two stripped wires hanging below the dash.
I took the driver's seat, kicked the clutch,
then eased again as I remembered
the glove box and the pint of Seagram's Billy Parker
had not broken the seal on. Like an alarm
the tree frogs went off in the woods. I drank
until they hushed
and I could hear through stray cricket chatter
the rockers on Billy Parker's chair
grinding ridges into his living room floor, worry
working on him like hard time. Then a wind
working in river grass, a red current
slicing around stumps and river snags, a boat-drift
pulling against an anchor
as I swayed in the seat of the black Camaro, grappled
for the two wires hanging in the darkness
between my knees, saw through the tinted windshield
by a sudden white moon rolling out of the clouds
a riverbank two counties away,
a wooden bridge, a place to jump
and roll on the soft shoulder of the gravel road,
a truck backed into a thicket a half-mile downstream.

L O U I S E   E R D R I C H

The Lady in the Pink Mustang

The sun goes down for hours, taking more of her along
than the night leaves her with.
A body moving in the dust
must shed its heavy parts in order to go on.

Perhaps you have heard of her, the Lady in the Pink Mustang,
whose bare lap is floodlit from under the dash,
who cruises beneath the high snouts of semis, reading
the blink of their lights. *Yes, Move Over. Now.*
or *How Much.* Her price shrinks into the dark.

She can't keep much trash in a Mustang,
and that's what she likes. Travel light. Don't keep
what does not have immediate uses. The road thinks ahead.
It thinks for her, a streamer from Bismarck to Fargo
bending through Minnesota to accommodate the land.

She won't carry things she can't use anymore.
Just a suit, sets of underwear, what you would expect
in a Pink Mustang. Things she could leave anywhere.

There is a point in the distance where the road meets itself,
where coming and going must kiss into one.
She is always at the place, seen from behind,
motionless, torn forward, living in a zone
all her own. It is like she has burned right through time,
the brand, the mark, owning the woman who bears it.

She owns them, not one will admit what they cannot
come close to must own them. She takes them along,
traveling light. It is what she must face every time
she is touched. The body disposable as cups.

To live, instead of turn, on a dime.
One light point that is so down in value.
Painting her nipples silver for a show, she is thinking
You out there. What do you know.

Come out of the dark where you're safe. Kissing these
bits of change, stamped out, ground to a luster,
is to kiss yourself away piece by piece
until we're even. Until the last
coin is rubbed for luck and spent.
I don't sell for nothing less.

KEVIN STEIN

Because You're American

You love the hum of a well-oiled engine about to turn 200,000, camera on passenger seat to shoot the ticker at 199,999.9, AM news announcing the Philippines has named a golf course in honor of John Paul II, not because the Pope plays but because his helicopter landed there and thus consecrated eighteenth green and clubhouse bar you're half a globe away from, wheeling through big bluestem, oak, and black locust to (no kidding) grandma's house beside the bridge where now an exaltation of white pelicans drifts the Des Moines River, central Iowa sudden late March exotic and you in wonder of America, what with pelicans in Iowa and bolus doses of vitamin C said to restore smokers' tarry lungs, though more research is needed to explain why white pelicans fish cooperatively like good little Marxists, lining up to beat their wings upon the water and drive fish to shallows for easy dining, which to your amazement they've begun to do while the car clicks toward 200,000.2, but the camera's in hand to get the pelicans in full collective display as the moment fritters away to Stephen Stills singing "Deja Vu" so why not pull off to snap the pelicans sparkling like crystal shards in a punch bowl, though a guy with an arm crutch clutters the foreground and it's best to wait until he clears the shot but he won't any time soon, left crutch plodding, right arm reaching back to yank right leg, shoulders and hips lurching to swivel and shudder ahead. Because this is America, the engine strums its oiled strings at a buck twenty-five a gallon, Barry Manilow oozes from the single muffled speaker, and the guy with crutch has covered a yard, maybe two, his face a proud saucer of water. There's "Chilly Billy" broadcasting from the brand new HoJo on I-80, free mugs and tee shirts, free rooms for seniors who've lost a spouse. Because this is America, there's stale Doublemint in the glove box, a black man in a Jeep stopping by the guy with crutch, who shakes his head, flaps his arm, then waves "Go on, go on" till the Jeep launches loose gravel like the rockets that protect us. There's grandma waiting, winners screaming madly over tickets to "Independence Day" and the DJ swearing he owns photos that prove we're not alone. There's "Deja Vu" all over again on Double Play Tuesday, joke as obscene as Stills' singing at Woodstock II. Because this is America, and you're American, you love the guy who reaches back to yank his leg, oh blessings, white pelicans in Iowa.

MARK WUNDERLICH

Take Good Care of Yourself

On the runway at the Rosy, the drag queen
fans herself gently, but with purpose.
She is an Asian princess, an elaborate wig
jangling like bells on a Shinto temple,
shoulders broad as my father's. With a flick

of her fan she covers her face, a whole
world of authority in that one gesture,
a screen sliding back, all black lacquer
and soprano laugh. The music of this place
echoes with the whip-crack of 2,000

men's libidos, and the one bitter pill
of X-tasy dissolving on my tongue is the perfect
slender measure of the holy ghost,
the vibe crawling my spine exactly,
I assure myself, what I've always wanted.

It is 1992. There is no you yet for me
to address, just simple imperative. *Give
me more. Give.* It is a vision, I'm sure
of this, of what heaven could provide—a sea
of men all muscle, white briefs and pearls,

of kilts cut too short for Catholic girls
or a Highland fling. Don't bother with chat
just yet. I've stripped and checked my jeans
at the door. I need a drink, a light, someplace
a little cooler, just for a minute, to chill.

There is no place like the unbearable ribbon
of highway that cuts the Midwest into two unequal
halves, a pale sun glowing like the fire
of one last cigarette. It is the prairie
I'm scared of, barreling off in all directions

flat as its inhabitants' A's and O's. I left
Wisconsin's well-tempered rooms
and snow-fields white and vacant as a bed
I'd wished I'd never slept in. Winters
I'd stare out the bus window through frost

at an icy template of what the world offered up—
the moon's tin cup of romance and a beauty,
that if held too long to the body,
would melt. If I'd felt anything for you then
it was mere, the flicker of possibility

a quickening of the pulse when I'd imagine
a future, not here but elsewhere, the sky
not yawning out, but hemmed in. In her dress
the drag is all glitter and perfect grace,
pure artifice, beating her fan, injuring

the smoky air, and in the club, I'm still
imagining. The stacks of speakers burn
and throb, whole cities of sound bear down
on us. I'm dancing with men all around me,
moving every muscle I can, the woman's voice

mixed and extended to a gorgeous black note
in a song that only now can I remember—
one familiar flat stretch, one wide-open vista
and a rhythm married to the words standing
for what it was we still had to lose.

LAWRENCE FERLINGHETTI

Lost Parents

It takes a fast car
        to lead a double life
in these days of short-distance love affairs
  when he has far-out lovers in
          three different locations
  and a date with each one
        at least twice a week
  a little simple arithmetic shows
    what a workout he's engaged in
  crossing & recrossing the city
    from bedroom to patio to swimming pool
the ignition key hot
    and the backseat a jumble of clothes
         for different life-styles
a surfboard on the roof
    and a copy of Kahlil Gibran or Rod McKuen
         under the dashboard
     next to the Indian music cassettes
   packs of Tarot and the I-Ching
         crammed into the glove compartment
  along with old traffic tickets
         and hardpacks of Kents
    dents attesting to the passion
        of his last lover
And his answering service
    catching him on the freeway

between two calls or two encounter groups
and the urgent message left

with an unlisted number to call Carol
about the bottle of fine wine
he forgot to pick up
and deliver to the gallery
for the reception at nine
While she shuttles to her gynecologist
and will meet him later
between two other numbers
male or female
including his wife
who also called twice
wanting to know where he's been
and what he's done
with their throw-away children
who
left to their own devices
in a beach house at Malibu
grew up and dropped out into Nothing
in a Jungian search
for lost parents
their own age

Scrabble

I was summoned to the porter's lodge for an overseas call from California. It was my girlfriend, who just wanted to say that she was fucking Jeff and they thought it best to tell me themselves, that I should have known a year away was no good for a relationship.

The porter, an old man with bad hearing, was rolling a cigarette and leaning in my direction. "No hard feelings. Okay, man?" said my ex-roommate. I hung up and went down to the pub. Some Americans from the basketball team were telling dirty jokes. I told one, too. We laughed and the next round was on me.

Hours later, trudging through the snow, I paused to chat with a Welsh acquaintance returning from his fiancée's. Under one arm he held a game, rubber band around the box, and he looked so happy and innocent that I had to cough, excuse myself and rush off.

Now, every year when I read his Christmas card, I remember him lambent with young love, material proof Good exists in the world. Oh, I know it's incredibly sentimental—I've grunted too long in the gutter not to recognize my own excess—but sometimes I think that if I could live again in that moment, rather than stumble down the street I would linger there in his presence, studying grace until I froze.

GARRETT HONGO

Off from Swing Shift

Late, just past midnight,
freeway noise from the Harbor
and San Diego leaking in
from the vent over the stove,
and he's off from swing shift at Lear's.
Eight hours of twisting circuitry,
charting ohms and maximum gains
while transformers hum
and helicopters swirl
on the roofs above the small factory.
He hails me with a head-fake,
then the bob and weave
of a weekend middleweight
learned at the Y on Kapiolani
ten years before I was born.

The shoes and gold London Fogger
come off first, then the easy grin
saying he's lucky as they come.
He gets into the slippers
my brother gives him every Christmas,
carries his Thermos over to the sink,
and slides into the one chair at the table
that's made of wood and not yellow plastic.
He pushes aside stacks
of *Sporting News* and *Outdoor Life*,
big round tins of Holland butter cookies,

and clears a space for his elbows, his pens,
and the *Racing Form*'s Late Evening Final.

His left hand reaches out,
flicks on the Sony transistor
we bought for his birthday
when I was fifteen.
The right ferries in the earphone,
a small, flesh-colored star,
like a tiny miracle of hearing,
and fits it into place.
I see him plot black constellations
of figures and calculations
on the magazine's margins,
alternately squint and frown
as he fingers the knob of the tuner
searching for the one band
that will call out today's results.

There are whole cosmologies
in a single handicap,
a lifetime of two-dollar losing
in one pick of the Daily Double.

Maybe tonight is his night
for winning, his night
for beating the odds
of going deaf from a shell
at Anzio still echoing
in the cave of his inner ear,
his night for cashing in
the blue chips of shrapnel still grinding
at the thickening joints of his legs.

But no one calls
the horse's name, no one
says Shackles, Rebate, or Pouring Rain.
No one speaks a word.

EMILY HIESTAND

Moon Winx Motel

Tuscaloosa, Alabama 1955

The Moon Winx with its neon eyes and sly smile
was the sure sign that our road trip South was over.
Only the apron of pale, rufous pebbles from the river,
and a driveway buckling under Goodyear tires
meant we were closer—to the Gothic radios, the yellowing
sheafs of sewing pattern tissues, the lenses
that magnified the Word of my mother's people.
Their driveways were paved in water worn pebbles:
a fluid pelt—acrid in heat, first powdered by drifting clays,
then washed by warm rains to the colors of salmon
and salamander. The stones could close as cool
and snug as a pocket around bare feet when we stood,
ankle-deep, in the one-time bed of the Tombigbee River.
There we made a game, called it Going to the Moon:
loop a rubber band on a gimcrack rocket;
shoot the cellophane ship into the sky;
then crane your neck—wowed by flight.
The land we learned to love was the land of the Creek
(rightly, the Muscogee Alliance), and it was dotted
with indigenous Coca-cola machines
aligned with perfect posture along shank ends
of brick motels and a la mode beauty salons.
Perhaps a poodle in the window. For our nickel,
we got the sweet brown wine of America: a formula

only recently revealed, by chance: it is solvent,
and caramel, oils of naroli, coriander, some lime,
and one unknown: the so-called, still secret: "7X."

LYNN EMANUEL

Outside Room Six

Down on my knees again, on the linoleum outside room six,
I polish it with the remnant of Grandpa's union suit,
and once again dead Grandma Fry looks down on me
from Paradise and tells me from the balcony of wrath
I am girlhood's one bad line of credit.

Every older girl I know is learning how to in a car,
while here I am, eye at the keyhole, watching Raoul,
who heats my dreams with his red hair, lights up my life
with his polished brogues, groans *Jesus, Jesus.*
I am little and stare into the dark until the whole small

town of lust emerges. I stare with envy, I stare and stare.
Now they are having cocktails. The drinks are dim lagoons
beneath their paper parasols. The air is stung with orange,
with lemon, a dash of Clorox, a dash of bitters;
black square, white square goes the linoleum.

GREG PAPE

In the Bluemist Motel

I hear voices in the next room
that stop and the closing of a door
in the Bluemist Motel in Florence, Arizona,
across the road from the state penitentiary,
where I am about to close the venetian blinds
to mute the light that shines all night
from the guard towers and the sign.
In this room, I imagine, two brothers
plotted the escape of their father
who had murdered a man in a rage
but had always loved his boys.
They made it almost to Gallup
before their stolen van was stopped
at a roadblock, just north of the Río Puerco
on Defiance Plateau, and the shooting began.
One of the boys took a bullet in the brain
and died there under the stars and shattered
glass. Now, the other brother and the father
live in separate cells across the road
and listen, as I do, at intervals all night
to the metallic voice of the loudspeaker
giving instruction in numbers and code.
This is years ago as I stand at the window
with the cord in my hand dusted blue
from the neon sign that buzzes over
the parking lot and the locked cars.

I don't know why all this comes back
tonight, insistent, as if I might
have done something to change the course
of these lives. As if I might have stepped in
between the father and the man he was about
to murder and said something strong and final
so that the father turned away in shame
and the sheriff never pulled the trigger
and the boy is still walking around somewhere
with a perfectly good brain he's finally
learning how to use, and his brother
has decided to marry again for the second
or third time and, because he's put in
a good day's work and he's tired, the father
is falling asleep in his own bed.

MARTÍN ESPADA

Transient Hotel Sky
at the Hour of Sleep

On the late shift, front desk,
midnight to 8 AM,
we watched the sky through crusted windows,
till the clouds swirled away
like water in the drain
of a steel sink.

In the clouded liquid light
human shapes would harden,
an Army jacket staggering
against the bannister at bartime,
coal-skinned man
drifting through the lobby
moaning to himself
about Mississippi,
a known arsonist
squeezing his head
in the microwave oven
with a giggle.

As we studied the white face
of the clock above the desk,
fluorescent hum of 4 AM,
a cowboy bragged
about buying good boots
for 19 cents from a retarded man,

then swaggered out the door
with a pickaxe
and a treasure map.
The janitor mopped the floor
nostalgic for Vietnam snapshots
confiscated at the airport,
peasant corpses with jaws
lopsided in a song of missing teeth.

Slowly the sky was a comfort,
like the pillow of a patient
sick for decades
and sleeping at last.
At the hour of sleep
a man called Johnson
trotted down the hallway
and leaned out the window,
then again, haunting
the fifth floor
in a staring litany
of gestures, so even
the security guard on rounds
wrote in the logbook for social workers
who never kept a schedule at night.
Johnson leaped
through the greasy pane of sky
at 5 AM,
refused suicide in flight,
and kicking struggled to stand in the air,
but snapped his ankles on the sidewalk
and burst his head on the curb,
scalp flapped open like the lid
on a bucket of red paint.

The newspaper shocked mouths
that day, but the transient hotel sky

drained pale as usual,
and someone pissed in the ashtray
by the desk, then leered
at the jabbering smokers.

PAUL ALLEN

Tattoo #47,
"Happy Dragon"

Through the crawl space
of the home that will have to do us,
at least until the kids go off,
trying to tighten the jacks
to shore up our giving floor,

I've pulled the light with the long cord
fed from inside loose. I didn't know
I had been staring at the blue dragon.
After nearly 30 years it sleeps deep
and dull under the scaly skin of my arm.
I hadn't thought I was looking at anything,
but in the surprising dark, the face lit,
lifted off my arm and went with my eyes
to the corners. Pensacola, '64, the only time
I did another guy. At Gulf's edge,

those early years, those treacherous
shallows of war—we drank too many beers
and walked away from town on his pass,
six-packs cooling our burning arms.
There was a fog, up or down the beach—
up, say—hovering head high.
It drew us in.
We laughed about something or other.

(He knew he was not coming back—
like all who went, or didn't.

Nobody ever made it back from then, I guess.)
Our too loud laughs hacked against the surf.
Foam spewed from our nostrils. We dropped
to our knees in the clear below the cloud,
saw for ourselves the long light
of water down the waves
to the lights we came from. He wept
because—I don't know why he wept.
Nor how we went from that to all the other.
Or how we sobered up enough to ever feel
our way back to familiar streets.

Light: My wife
has found the pulled plug in our bedroom.
Screw it—that, and that war, wars to come.
Screw the jacks up tighter to the frame.
Dragon's as dull as ever, dim as I'd remembered—
should have had the tacky thing removed,
except the scar. "Number 47, 'Happy Dragon'":
You never drink so much you forget a thing like that,
like your own voice ordering your own tattoo.
I'm not sure what that other fellow chose.

SANDRA McPHERSON

Pornography, Nebraska

Once, on that highway where a traveler works hard
To remember what he loves intensely in this life,
    Because it is so endlessly bare,
    The highway I mean,

I heard on our CB one trucker tell another
About tattoos around the areolas. About the hurt.
    The second man's
    Hadn't been as bad, but needling him elsewhere—

To recall a barberpole—
Caused definitive pain. Drunk when he started,
    He couldn't renege until the last prick of ink.
    It was sobering.

On this long journey out of cultivation, sage
At last outspices hay. Bulls twist up dust
    In an hourglass-shaped battle,
    Heads at the center.

A vulture on a fencepost
Like a single staked rose by a farmhouse . . .
    And still the voice of public confession
    Goes through the dotty illustrations on his body,

Forty-some, he says, like milemarkers to the border.
Then I remember losing him,
    If only on the radio.
    It was at last so dark I felt the way I did

When once I was actually leaving someone I dearly loved.
Moonlight traveled
    The bedspring spiral of my notebook
    In which I recorded the distance

From him by the fuel burned.
Wherever the pictured man was, somewhere a spanker
    Like "PJ's" back in Muscatine
    Performed astonished love

As a way of testing out his story, seeing
If she could believe him.
    New voices
    Took over the channel

But they only tattled on a patrol,
Who soon appeared, his outwitted chase-light off.
    Then one last voice—
    A siren at the stateline,

Crying higher, calling out.
It involved catching no one. Lightning
    Had fired the ranges. All the Pine Bluffs,
    Wyoming, Fire Department volunteers

Stopped dreaming. They knew they must cool
Their nakedness; the wail said they must drive,
    As fast as they could,
    Away from their beds.

DAVID BOTTOMS

In a U-Haul North of Damascus

1.

Lord, what are the sins
I have tried to leave behind me? The bad checks,
the workless days, the scotch bottles thrown across the fence
and into the woods, the cruelty of silence,
the cruelty of lies, the jealousy,
the indifference?

What are these on the scale of sin
or failure
that they should follow me through the streets of Columbus,
the moon-streaked fields between Benevolence
and Cuthbert where dwarfed cotton sparkles like pearls
on the shoulders of the road. What are these
that they should find me half-lost,
sick and sleepless
behind the wheel of this U-Haul truck parked in a field
    on Georgia 45
a few miles north of Damascus,
some makeshift rest stop for eighteen wheelers
where the long white arms of oaks slap across trailers
and headlights glare all night through a wall of pines?

2.

What was I thinking, Lord?
That for once I'd be in the driver's seat, a firm grip
on direction?

So the jon boat muscled up the ramp,
the Johnson outboard, the bent frame of the wrecked Harley
chained for so long to the back fence,
the scarred desk, the bookcases and books,
the mattress and box springs,
a broken turntable, a Pioneer amp, a pair
of three-way speakers, everything mine
I intended to keep. Everything else abandon.

But on the road from one state
to another, what is left behind nags back through the distance,
a last word rising to a scream, a salad bowl
shattering against a kitchen cabinet, china barbs
spiking my heel, blood trailed across the cream linoleum
like the bedsheet that morning long ago
just before I watched the future miscarried.

Jesus, could the irony be
that suffering forms a stronger bond than love?

3.

Now the sun
streaks the windshield with yellow and orange, heavy beads
of light drawing highways in the dew-cover.
I roll down the window and breathe the pine-air,
the after-scent of rain, and the far-off smell
of asphalt and diesel fumes.
But mostly pine and rain
as though the world really could be clean again.

Somewhere behind me,
miles behind me on a two-lane that streaks across
west Georgia, light is falling
through the windows of my half-empty house.
Lord, why am I thinking about this? And why should I care
so long after everything has fallen
to pain that the woman sleeping there should be sleeping alone?
Could I be just another sinner who needs to be blinded
before he can see? Lord, is it possible to fall
toward grace? Could I be moved
to believe in new beginnings? Could I be moved?

ALBERTO RÍOS

The Man She Called Honey, and Married

In her hands she holds
purple blossoms inside
under her sailor-white skin
like a tattoo, like tattoos all over
of the Virgin of Guadalupe and Christ
too old now to have a face
or a body, just pieces of them now
huge on her forearms
and her face,
bigger almost
bursting out larger in some places
than the skin to hold them,
no room in her small eyes
to see more
than these purple flowers and
black and yellow,
bouquets smelling greenhouse hot inside
behind her eyes, in the pit of her head
smelling with her eyes
drawing the breath of pain
through them
into herself, into her small center
for one hard moment like a man,
a sailor, was a sailor, tattooed

and the long second he took
to put his pictures on her
with his hands.

MATTHEW ROHRER

After the Wedding Party

The sun set early on the forest
of coffee-stirrers,
on the cold-blooded buildings,
churches among them.

The light bent back the branches,
where a mockingbird purled
like a hack on trombone.
I was involved in a physical act
I was unable to understand
—in love, but also walking back
to the dining car on a train going 80 miles an hour.
I strongly believed the Truth was a fixed point
in the trees, watching me travel
through the southern nightfall
backwards recklessly. I misunderstood.
My lover cradled a camera
to her weakened eyes—"I want
to take a picture of where the night
just was." Common decency forbade me
from expressing my love
down her shirt under the mothering eye
of a town's watertower.
The tower said "Smile America"
and "I plugged Heather Griggs."

TIMOTHY LIU

Ikon

Nothing comforts me, not Gloria Swanson
in a black-and-white toque, nor Colette
reclining on a red divan, her chin at rest
near the edge of a table with flowers on it.
No matter where I stand, spindled postcards
in an all-night diner, tins of custard pie
vanishing from the counter while faces
come alive, mercy in the sound of quarters
being dropped into a jukebox. The songs I know
but cannot sing remind me of a stranger
who undid my khaki trousers in the back
of an eighteen-wheeler, who said he wanted
to fuck me with a crowbar while kissing
the face of Christ he kept inside his wallet.

PAUL ALLEN

Pickup

"I love my truck. . . ."
—Glen Campbell

Sometimes there has been enough writing.

A tall one between my legs, plenty of smokes,
squelch off, hammer down, we're on the I
again in Alabama. This is country country
on WBAM coming to you live, neighbor.

The boy I found in Montgomery
hitchhiking with my old thumb
strikes a match to show me
L.I.F.E.
tattooed on each knuckle of his left fist
with a Bic pen in the state pen.
Another match, miles down, lights
his right wrist: *Can you read*
it? Read what this one says.
I'm driving. I can't read it.
Thirteen and a half, 13 ¹/₂ is what. I unlock
my beer from my legs and suck the last foam.
Know what it means? You got this red truck,
and I can tell you got a real family
so you don't know what it means.
I tell him he's right. I don't know.
Twelve man jury, one judge,
and a half-ass chance. Twelve, one, a half.

[314]

Keith tells me for ten bucks he'll fight
me, for twenty I can love him
up some, for fifty, he'll go down
on me, *but my private life*
about my brother and my uncle
and my old man being charged
with kidnapping me is nobody
else's business, so don't ask.
Just don't by-God ask. I won't talk personal.
We shake hands on it.

He looks at me to the next yard stick,
mile marker 109.
He shifts his feet in the maps,
coffee cups, beer cans.
I was in for a year and nine months.
They picked me up in Alabama,
but I did my time in Florida.
Gainesville?

Gainesville, what?
The night begins to change. The hour
before light. Back home
my girls—wife, two daughters, a fixed cat—
are locked in with the alarm armed.
They would not dream I have found this Keith.
Up ahead a flatbed hauls a house.

I don't know about no Gainesville.
I just know I was somewhere in Florida.
But see, it was dark when the state delivered me
and it was dark when they took me home.
So I don't know. Might be like you say. Might
have been Gainesville. I'm always getting
screwed over by The Man,
so it might have been someplace else.

I like you, but you don't know everything.
It might have been someplace you don't know.

He takes the off-ramp at Ft. Deposit
where a man owes him money.
Hey. If you write about me and tonight
and me riding with you in your red truck,
I hope you make a million dollars.

The house passes us.
I pop another beer and head on south,
find my station again.
Damn fine truck—
my Beatrice. My Linda Ronstadt.
My whining wide red woman.

Author Index

Title Index

First Line Index

[325]

Acknowledgments

Despite our efforts, we were able to reach neither the poets nor the publishers of a very few works represented in this anthology.

Ai. "Blue Suede Shoes" by Ai, from *Sin* (Houghton Mifflin Co., 1986).

Sherman Alexie. "November 22, 1983" reprinted from *The Business of Fancydancing* © 1992 by Sherman Alexie. Used by permission of the author and Hanging Loose Press.

Paul Allen. "Pickup" and "Tattoo #47, 'Happy Dragon'," reprinted from *American Crawl* (University of North Texas Press) by Paul Allen. © Paul Allen. Reprinted by permission of the author.

Paula Gunn Allen. "Teaching Poetry at Votech High, Santa Fe, the Week John Lennon Was Shot," from *Life Is a Fatal Disease: Collected Poems 1962–1995* (University of New Mexico Press) by Paula Gunn Allen © 1996. Reprinted by permission of the author.

David Baker. "8-Ball at the Twilite" is reprinted from *Haunts*, published by Cleveland State University, and appears courtesy of the author.

Peter Balakian. "The End of the Reagan Era" from *Dyer's Thistles*, by Peter Balakian © 1996. Reprinted by permission of the author and Carnegie Mellon University Press.

Dorothy Barresi. "When I Think about America Sometimes (I Think of Ralph Kramden)" from *The Post-Rapture Diner* by Dorothy Barresi © 1996. Reprinted by permission of the author and The University of Pittsburgh Press.

Robin Becker. "Dreaming at the Rexall Drug" and "Peter Pan in North America" from *All-American Girl* by Robin Becker © 1996. Reprinted by permission of the author and The University of Pittsburgh Press.

Angela Jackson. "Billie in Silk," from *Dark Legs and Silk Kisses* (Triquarterly Books) by Angela Jackson.

Lori Jakiela. "A Personal History of Hands," by Lori Jakiela first appeared in *Chicago Review*. Reprinted by permission of the author.

Denis Johnson. "The Incognito Lounge," from *The Incognito Lounge and Other Poems* by Denis Johnson © 1994. Reprinted by permission of Carnegie Mellon University Press.

Markham Johnson. "The All-Night Diner," from *Collecting the Light* (University Press of Florida) by Markham Johnson © 1992. Reprinted by permission of the author.

Patricia Spears Jones. "If I Were Rita Hayworth" and "The Birth of Rhythm and Blues," from *The Weather That Kills* by Patricia Spears Jones © 1995. Reprinted by permission of the author and Coffee House Press.

Rodney Jones. "On the Bearing of Waitresses," from *Transparent Gestures*. Copyright © 1989 by Rodney Jones. Reprinted by permission of the author and Houghton Mifflin Co. All rights reserved. "TV," from *Things That Happen Once*. Copyright © 1996 by Rodney Jones. Reprinted by permission of the author and Houghton Mifflin Co. All rights reserved.

June Jordan. "Mid-Year Report: For Haruko" by June Jordan first appeared in *Iowa Review* 26.2. © June Jordan. Reprinted by permission of the author.

klipschutz. "Funicello at 50" by klipschutz from *Spoon River Poetry Review* 22.1 (Winter/Spring 1997). Reprinted by permission of the author and *Spoon River Poetry Review*.

Yusef Komunyakaa. "Never Land" by Yusef Komunyakaa, from *Chicago Review* 40.2 & 3. Reprinted by permission of the author and *Chicago Review*.

Mary A. Koncel. "Come Back, Elvis, Come Back to Holyoke" by Mary A. Koncel, first appeared in *Illinois Review*. © Mary A. Koncel. Reprinted by permission of the author and *Illinois Review*.

Bill Kushner. "Up," from *Head* (United Artists Books) by Bill Kushner. © 1986 Bill Kushner. Reprinted by permission of the author and United Artists Books.

David Lehman. "The Difference between Pepsi and Coke," from *An Alternative to Speed* (Princeton University Press) by David Lehman © 1986. Reprinted by permission of the author.

Pamela Stewart. "Punk Pantoum" by Pamela Stewart first appeared in *Crazy Horse* (Spring 1979). Reprinted by permission of the author and *Crazy Horse*.

Susan Swartwout. "The Gypsy Teaches Her Grandchild Wolfen Ways" by Susan Swartwout. Reprinted by permission of the author. "Siamese Twins in Love," from *Freaks* by Susan Swartwout. Reprinted by permission of the author and Dillon Press.

Janet Sylvester. "Arrowhead Christian Center and No-Smoking Luncheonette," from *That Mulberry Wine* (Wesleyan University Press) by Janet Sylvester. Reprinted by permission of the author.

Thom Tammaro. "'mericn fst fd" © by Thom Tammaro, from *Chicago Review*. Reprinted by permission of the author.

Luci Tapahonso. "Pay Up or Else," from *Seasonal Woman* by Luci Tapahonso. Reprinted by permission of the author.

James Tate. "The Motorcyclists," from *Selected Poems* by James Tate (Wesleyan University Press). © 1991 by James Tate. Reprinted by permission of University Press of New England and the author.

David Trinidad. "The Shower Scene in *Psycho*," from *Answer Song* (High Risk Books, 1994). © 1994 by David Trinidad. Reprinted by permission of the author.

William Trowbridge. "Kong Breaks a Leg at the William Morris Agency" and "Viet Kong," from *Enter Dark Stranger* by William Trowbridge. Reprinted by permission of the author and the University of Arkansas Press.

Kitty Tsui. "Suzy Wong's Been Dead a Long Time" by Kitty Tsui first appeared in *Iowa Review* 26.2. © Kitty Tsui. Reprinted by permission of the author.

Tino Villanueva. "Scene from the Movie *Giant*," from *Scene from the Movie "Giant"* by Tino Villanueva © 1988.

Paul Violi. "Harold and Imogene" by Paul Violi reprinted by permission of the author.

Gale Renée Walden. "Misguided Angels," from *Same Blue Chevy* by Gale Renée Walden. Reprinted by permission of the author.

Charles H. Webb. "Rumpelstiltskin Convention" by Charles H. Webb. Published in *Laurel Review* 30.2 (Summer 1996). Reprinted by permission of the author and *Laurel Review*.